GunDigest
SHOOTER'S GUIDE to
RELOADING

D1733376

PHILIP P. MASSARO

Published by

Gun Digest® Books, an imprint of F+W Media, Inc.
Krause Publications • 700 East State Street • Iola, WI 54990-0001
715-445-2214 • 888-457-2873
www.krausebooks.com

To order books or other products call toll-free 1-800-258-0929
or visit us online at www.gundigeststore.com

ISBN-13: 978-1-4402-3988-5
ISBN-10: 1-4402-3988-6

Edited by Jennifer L.S. Pearsall
Cover Design by Dane Royer and Nicole MacMartin
Designed by Nicole MacMartin

Printed in USA

DEDICATION

This book is dedicated to the men and women who have given life and limb in the defense of the United States of America, and thereby given us all the opportunity to enjoy the use of our firearms as a free people. It is a debt that cannot be repaid, and I personally wish to express my sincere gratitude to them.

ABOUT THE AUTHOR

Philip P. Massaro is the President of Massaro Ballistic Laboratories, LLC, a custom ammunition company comfortably nestled in between the Hudson River and Catskill Mountains of upstate New York. He has been handloading ammunition for more than 20 years and has created a wide range of pistol and rifle ammunition from the lightest plinking loads through the heaviest-hitting cartridges designed for animals that are measured in tons. Having been taught how to shoot as a very young man, he soon developed a love for firearms and their paraphernalia. He is a veteran of three African safaris and dozens of North American hunts, and enjoys quality time spent afield in the quiet, wild places. He is a Licensed Professional Land Surveyor by trade, a musician by choice, and usually reeks of Hoppes No. 9.

ACKNOWLEDGEMENTS

As with any book that pertains to a specific field, there are a multitude of influences that gives an author the initiative to take on the task in the first place. Reloading is no different.

I'd first like to pay homage to those who gave birth to the industry as we know it. Names like Bruce Hodgdon, Vernon Speer, Joyce Hornady, John Nosler, Bill Hober, and too many more to name have provided us with the building blocks to make great ammunition. Then there are those who have built the tools we use during every reloading session. The great folks at RCBS, Redding, Hornady, Lyman, Lee, Forster, Dillon, et al, make our job of creating good ammunition not only possible, but much easier, as time goes on.

Then there's the writing end of things. Honestly, I am a reloader who writes, not a writer who reloads. There are many authors who have mesmerized me for countless hours with their stories, be it about hunting or reloading. Roosevelt, Hemingway, Ruark, Capstick, and so many others are certainly among those who've intrigued me with their talk of hunting adventure and firearms facts. Of them all, there is one writer who's held my attention for decades, and I've been fortunate enough to call him a friend. Craig Boddington, thank you for all the encouraging words, both in print and in conversation.

And, there are those in the industry who make the author's life easier by simply being available to discuss and explain. Chris Hodgdon of Hodgdon Powders, Bill Hober of Swift Bullets, Randy Brooks of Barnes Bullets, the good folks at North Fork Bullets, Carroll Pillant of Sierra, Kent Sakamoto at RCBS, and last but most certainly not least, my friend Robin Sharpless at Redding Reloading Products, have all helped in the gathering and presenting of this information. Gentlemen, I raise my glass to you.

Last, there are those in your life who help to shape things along the way. I was taught to reload by my dad, Philip J. Massaro. He's a damned good handloader in his own right, and I'd like to thank him for showing me what goes where. Donald B. Thorne, Jr., USMC, known better as Col. Le Frogg, broke me from the thought mold of one caliber, one bullet, one powder. I'd like to thank you, Le Frogg, for being a mentor and a second father to me, and for showing me the wide world of rifle and pistol calibers. J.D. Fielding, whose images are throughout this book, and who is a wonderful human to work with. My pals Dave de Moulpied, Mark "Pig-Newton" Nazi, Marty Groppi, Steve Darling, Jarrett Lane, Bill Loëb, and Kevin Hicks, thank you gents for the countless hours spent talking boldly, as men do, about guns, hunting and reloading. And special thanks to my wife, Suzie, who has been so supportive during the hours I've sat in front of the computer keyboard, wondering if I could really do this. I love you sweetie.—*Philip P. Massaro*

FOREWORD

This is Phil Massaro's first book. This fact is important not so that we can forgive any imperfections or lack of completeness; these may or may not be present, but, after all, Webster's Dictionary is still a work in progress. Absolute perfection and total completeness, regardless one's first book or last book, are impossibly beyond reach and cannot be expected.

Undoubtedly, there are some things you or I may wish had been included and, since *The Gun Digest Shooter's Guide to Reloading* is very much a hands-on, how-to book, there may even be things we might do differently. It's perfectly okay to disagree, but let's keep in mind that this is Phil Massaro's book, not yours or mine. That said, it is a *complete* book, a valuable tool for anyone interested in improving their reloading techniques and repertoire, and improving the performance of their firearms. The methodology is sound and up to date, and Phil's knowledge of the subject is clearly there.

I have written many books over a long career, but I would be the first to say that this is not a book I could write. I started handloading about 1964, the same year I saw the Beatles on their first tour (I put that in because, although Phil is also an accomplished musician, he's a bit too young to have seen the Beatles!). My family was comprised of shotgunners and bird hunters who had absolutely no familiarity with centerfire rifles, so Dad turned me over to a friend, Jack Pohl, of the old E.C. Bishop and Sons gunstock company in Warsaw, Missouri ("Gunstock Capitol of the World" said the sign on the city limits). The deal was that before Jack would teach me (and Dad) rifle shooting, we had to first learn how to reload.

The propellants were post-World War II bulk from Hodgdon, stored in smoky glass jars, but the principles of the practice were pretty much the same, as were the most basic tools. A major difference, of course, is that today have a lot more powders, bullets, and primers to choose from than we did back then, along with a bewildering array of data. A more subtle difference is that precision techniques and specialized tools have advanced tremendously in the last half-century. I freely admit that I have made no effort to keep up—so there is no way I could even attempt to write this book. Phil Massaro could, though, and did. He is at the same time both a student and professor of reloading, master of the classical form of the art, and experimenter in the emerging technological alchemy. Although I've been doing this stuff for a very long time, this is a book I will learn from and often refer back to.

I stated at the beginning that this was Phil's first book. This is important for him, because a first book is a major milestone for any writer. It is a long and grueling process, and the first book is the hardest of all. It begins with the seemingly impossible task of convincing a publisher that you have something to say. In fact Phil Massaro does have something to say—quite a lot and of value, as you will see. Ah, but once having made the sale, the writer now has to produce the goods. As he sets to the task, he reminds himself constantly to "be careful what you wish for." It seems like it will never be finished, and, indeed, many books that are started are never finished. This one obviously was, and it's a good book, full of valuable information on its subject.

This last is why the book is important to you—but it should also be important to you that this is Phil Massaro's first book, because I am certain it will not be his last! I met Phil at the massive Harrisburg Sports Show a few years back. I liked him, and what's not to like? Still a young man, I found him energetic, passionate, and amazingly knowledgeable about shooting and hunting. We've traded information back and forth, and I've called upon his Massaro Ballistics Laboratories to solve some vexing ammo problems—with consistently superb results. He knows his stuff.

The Gun Digest publishing house has presented many books from many writers for many years. So it is and should be expected that Phil knows his stuff. That is almost a given. Here's the challenge: This is not a subject that is easy to write about, nor is it normally easy to read. Let's face it, reloading, though an enjoyable and rewarding pastime, is a fairly dry subject! Even with the required detailed knowledge (which Phil surely has), technical stuff is hard to write and harder to make enjoyable to read. This is a difference that you will find in this book, Phil Massaro's first (but surely not his last).

When I met Phil, he told me he was doing some writing and would like to do more. Of course, I hear that a lot, but I liked him and offered what encouragement I could. He had the technical knowledge and the passion, two great prerequisites in this specialized field, but here's what I didn't realize for a while: He also has the talent! His writing is lively and fresh, bringing both feeling and humor to a subject that has traditionally been dealt with in staid, textbook fashion. Because of that, because of Phil, you will not only learn from this book, you will enjoy it. This, I suspect, will make you refer back to it more often, rendering this book even more useful. Whether a first or last book, *The Gun Digest Shooters Guide to Reloading* is, thus, a milestone work on the subject: Not only packed with useful information, but also readable and thus even more useful. I am very pleased that it's his first book rather than his last, because I am convinced that we will be reading—and enjoying—a lot more Phil Massaro in years to come!—*Craig Boddington*

CONTENTS

INTRODUCTION

Once upon a time, a little boy watched his father sort out the spent brass casings from his .308 Winchester, after returning from a trip to the shooting range to sight in the rifle for the upcoming deer season. The questions came forth immediately.

"Dad, why are you saving those?"

"Because you can reload them and shoot them again."

"Dad, can we do that?"

"Yes we can. I'll have to pick up some bullets, powder, and primers."

"Dad, can we do that now? *Pleeeeeeeease?*"

As you can see, this youth was enamored with the idea of spending time with his father making ammunition (he still is), and he had an immediate thirst for knowledge of the subject. Long tale made short, the boy and his dad did make those .308s come alive again and, when the little guy got to be a bigger guy, a love affair with both firearms and the experimentation with ammunition would just about drive his father off the deep end.

That boy is me. I say is, and not was, because I've never lost that boyhood feeling of excitement when it comes to creating special ammunition that cannot be purchased, whether it's a plinking load for a pistol or some dangerous-game ammunition that gets me one step closer to being in the hunting fields I love so much. I still get excited about the polished gold or silver colored cases, the sharp tips of spitzer bullets, the parallel-sided solids, and the mystique of hunting strange places with stranger names, with these components in hand.

This book is a how-to manual, in that, when you are done reading it, you will know the basic principles and proper methods of loading a centerfire pistol or rifle cartridge. I also hope that it inspires the reader to further probe into the endless possibilities, when it comes to choosing a combination of bullet and powder that will make you proud and con-fident in your choice of firearm. Reloading ammunition gives the shooter an opportunity to spend additional time at the range with their guns, and that enhances the bond between the shooter and the tools they use.

While most instructional manuals can be legally classified as a cure for insomnia, *The Gun Digest Shooter's Guide to Reloading* was written in an attempt to convey the techni-cal message in a real-world manner based on real-world experiences; I've done my best to demystify some of the scarier terminology and nomenclature associated with ammunition and the practice of reloading it. This book is not designed to standalone. It will require the wealth of information found in the quality reloading manuals published by others to be fully useful. Yet this book will be very helpful in clearly and simply explaining the reload-ing processes and get you out of trouble should something go awry. Too, if you have already been a loader for some time, you may find some helpful tips and new products that are available to whet your appetite within these pages. For those new to it all, please soak it in and enjoy your new hobby!—*Philip P. Massaro*

CHAPTER 1

A RELOADING OVERVIEW:
Why Do I Want To Do This?

Reloading is a highly rewarding activity. (Photo courtesy Massaro Media Group & J.D. Fielding Photography)

It happens often. I'll be at a party or some type of gathering, and one of the crew starts talking about reloading. We're gun folks, it's like that. If more than one of the crew is assembled, it gets pretty deep. There have been nights where Mark "Pig-Newton" Nazi (yes, that's really his last name), Marty Groppi, and I end up in a conversation that sounds like Chinese algebra to the bystander. Folks look on in wonder (or is it pity?) as we debate powder burn rates and sectional densities and idly prattle on about secant ogives. I must admit, it's a bit nerdy, but once you take the plunge into the world of creating and controlling your own

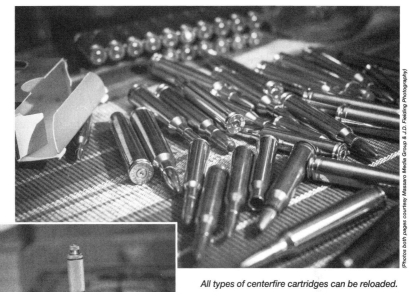

All types of centerfire cartridges can be reloaded.

(Photos both pages courtesy Massaro Media Group & J.D. Fielding Photography)

The process of reloading a rifle cartridge.

language and mathematics that can make so many shooters feel dizzy at the thought of reloading. I shall do my best to explain it plainly, without you either running for the hills or nodding off.

The first question you may have is "Why would I want to reload?" Good question, because today's factory ammunition is good stuff, hands down. It's available in many different calibers and with the choice of many different bullets. But not all rifles or pistols perform well with factory ammunition. Some give poor accuracy. Others give a level of recoil that is unpleasant. With custom ammunition, handloaded by you, both accuracy and speed (and, therefore, recoil), can be tailored to suit your needs.

Reloading can be likened to a suit of clothing: Sometimes a suit fits just right off the rack, while other times you're going to look and feel your

ammunition, it can be downright addicting. It will help you better understand your firearms and how to better use the right tool for the shooting situation at hand. Also, know that if you're already terrified after reading the phrases "sectional densities" and "secant ogives," rest assured that, within the covers of this book, I hope to dispel much of the arcane best with a suit that is custom-made to your measurements and in the style and color you like. I get a sense of pride when I take the walk to the target board and see good accuracy and tight groups, or when I cleanly and quickly take an animal in the hunting fields with ammunition of my own creation.

Another reason to reload is that many hunters and shooters own and enjoy rifles and pistols that are chambered for cartridges the ammunition companies have dropped from their product lines. Then what? Well, don't retire that gun so quickly! By purchasing the necessary tools and components, you can make a lifetime supply of ammo for your old sweetheart. My dear friend and mentor, Donald B. Thorne, Jr., USMC, better known as "Colonel Le Frogg," has a Winchester Model 70 rifle he loves, one that's chambered in the venerable .264 Winchester Magnum. This is a wonderful cartridge, but long ago lost the popularity contest to the 7mm Remington Magnum; subsequently, factory ammunition for this round was dropped by most ammunition companies. Le Frogg ordered a bunch of cases, some suitable bullets, and reloading dies. Together, he and I created all the ammunition he will ever need. As a custom ammunition shop, my company Massaro Ballistic Laboratories has been honored to provide some rarities to our clients, so they can enjoy their older or near-obsolete firearms. With the guidance contained in this book, you can do the same for yourself.

Cases are invaluable to the reloader. (Photos both pages courtesy Massaro Media Group & J.D. Fielding Photography)

Reloading, also known as hand-loading, is the process of creating ammunition. Sometimes this means using spent casings, which you'll need to reform to their original specifications. Sometimes reloading means you're assembling all new components. It's a rewarding hobby either way and one that allows you to spend time with friends and loved ones. I learned from my father, good ol' Grumpy Pants, and have made many friends and acquaintances while discussing the various aspects of loading ammunition. In fact, Massaro Ballistic Laboratories came to fruition after many years of hobby handloading all sorts of rifle and pistol ammunition for family and friends. You can learn, too, and, as long as you are careful and diligent, you'll have a great time doing it!

Reloading is cost effective, another reason to give this an honest try. Let's face it, premium ammunition has become very expensive, and that's when you can find it at all. For many years, I have created my own premium ammunition for target shooting and hunting, at a fraction of the cost of purchasing factory stuff. The bigger calibers (which I really enjoy shooting) are particularly expensive to buy. Some of my safari rifles shoot cartridges that cost more than $200 per box of 20 rounds! Only through handloading could I afford to practice and hunt with these rifles. Those of you who enjoy time at the shooting range can shoot more often when ammunition is more economical. And more time shooting is a very good thing!

A box of Massaro Ballistic Laboratories .270 Winchester Short Magnum ammunition. MBL is a custom handloader, and what the folks there do, you can, too.

(Photos both pages courtesy Massaro Media Group & J.D. Fielding Photography)

Instruction at the bench. It's always helpful if you have an experienced reloader who can help you through your first rounds and troubleshoot any problems you might have with your initial press setup.

Introducing new shooters, including youngsters and the many women who are learning to enjoy the shooting sports these days, can be a frustrating proposition for both instructor and student, when the recoil of the firearm is too severe to promote good technique. The handloader can produce reduced-velocity ammunition that will allow the new shooter to ease into the feel of the rifle or pistol and develop good habits and shooting skills.

By handloading and developing the proper loads for your particular

Left to right, the author, Colonel Le Frogg, and his father, a.k.a. Grumpy Pants, discussing some new handloaded ammunition for their next hunt.

firearms, you not only create ammunition that is best suited for the shooting situation at hand, you become much more confident in your gun. The added time spent at the bench developing these loads will allow you to become much more familiar (and therefore safe!) with your chosen firearms, work out any potential hardware problems along the way, and may make the difference when the trophy of your dreams presents itself or when those precious tenths of a second mean the difference in the gun games. Gaining a thorough knowledge of your chosen cartridge's capabilities by loading the ammunition for it will certainly be an aid in maximizing the potential of your rifle or handgun. Seeing the repeatable results produced by consistent handloads will allow you to settle in

behind the sights of your firearm and know that you have a combination of gun and ammunition that shoots like an extension of your arm. That's something invaluable to me.

A thorough knowledge of reloading can also help aid in the choice of future firearms. Knowing the ballistics of a myriad of cartridges, as listed in any good reloading manual, will help you sift through the old wives' tales and rhetoric about the performance of certain rounds. With that knowledge replacing myth, you'll be well educated and fully capable of making an independent decision to purchase the firearms that best suit your needs.

Finally, there are often times you simply can't purchase the cartridge/bullet combination you envision. Sure, there are lots of choices available, hundreds even, but, if, you want a particular new whiz-bang bullet in a cartridge you are simply enamored with, you may have no choice other than to assemble it yourself. I've had the privilege of working with several professional hunters, in conjunction with major bullet manufacturers, to create ammunition for specific purposes, including the hunt for dangerous game. This ammunition is not available in stores, but our handloads suit the purpose at hand perfectly.

As I write these words, in the fall of 2013, we shooters are experiencing the biggest ammunition shortage in living memory. Store shelves are bare, ammunition is back-ordered, and though the ammunition factories are running at full capacity, the demand seems still to be growing faster. Reloading your own ammunition is a means of making sure you always have a supply of ammunition on hand for your firearms. Powder and primers need to be purchased, but cases can be reused. Bullets can even be cast from lead.

I'll break down the process in detail in the chapters that follow, but, for the present, here's the basic process of creating a single round of ammunition:

A cartridge case, if previously fired, must be resized back to its original dimensions. This is accomplished with "reloading dies," with the mechanical advantage of a "reloading press." Once the case is properly sized, the spent primer is removed and a new one is installed. An appropriate powder charge is then poured into the case and the new bullet seated. It's that simple. It is also infinitely complex, when you start to get into the subtle nuances and customize the performance of your handgun or rifle. There are many rules and details, which we will discuss, but that's the general gist of it.

The particular reloading setup you choose can be as simple or complex as you choose to make it. It does require a particular level of respect (gunpowder is a highly flammable substance), diligent record keeping, and your *undivided* attention. We will cover the components, the tools needed, the physics of this process, some helpful hints and scenarios, new products available, and many other points in the pages to come. So, have a seat, and allow me to introduce you to the world of reloading. Promise, we'll have some fun.

CHAPTER 2

THE CARTRIDGE COMPONENTS

The components, in exploded view.

(Photos courtesy Massaro Media Group & J.D. Fielding Photography)

THE CARTRIDGE CASE

The brass cartridge case is simply a combustion chamber. It holds the primer, powder charge, and bullet and withstands the forces of firing. It is a rugged, durable means of loading and reloading a rifle or pistol. The cartridge, fully assembled, is loaded into the rifle's or pistol's chamber; the gun's mechanism securely locks the cartridge in place by means of a bolt, breech, falling block, or cylinder. When the trigger is pulled and the gun's hammer comes forward, the primer is struck by the firing pin, sending a shower of sparks through its flash hole and into the powder charge. The resulting combustion creates a pressure level that forces the bullet to leave by its only point of escape, out of the cartridge and down the barrel. What you are left with is a an empty cartridge case (holding the now spent primer), which is now expanded to a mirror image of the chamber. The cartridge case is the only component of this process that can be reshaped and reused.

CARTRIDGE FIRING SEQUENCE

1. Firing Pin crushes priming compound against internal anvil, sending sparks through flash hole into the powder charge.

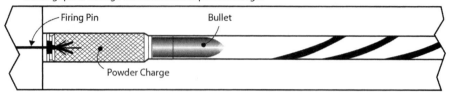

2. Powder Charge burnes, creating pressure from combustion.

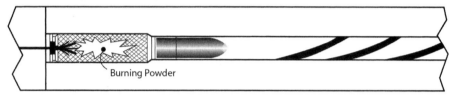

3. Pressure sends bullet down the barrel, the only means of escape.

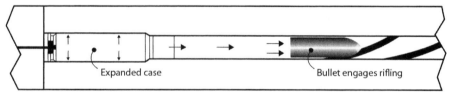

4. Case is expanded against chamber walls.

The simple, yet effective cartridge case.

All standardized cartridges in the U.S. are approved and regulated by SAAMI, the Sporting Arms and Ammunition Manufacturers' Institute (www.saami.org). Founded in 1926, this organization defines the standards and specifications for a particular cartridge. These standards include precise dimensioning and pressure limits. SAAMI offers highly detailed drawings of most any case it's approved, which can aid you in case preparation and resizing.

Most of the reloadable cartridge cases in use today are made of brass or nickel-coated brass. Brass is used because it is a malleable metal and can be reformed many times before it becomes brittle and cracks.

Although brass is malleable, it tarnishes easily, especially in wet weather or when handled frequently by sweaty hands (the salt and acids in your sweat tarnishes brass). This led to the development of nickel-coated brass. Nickel is still malleable enough to be formed and resized, but it doesn't tarnish. I like nickel brass, but the only caveat I would offer to using such cases is that nickel brass can scratch conventional reloading dies after prolonged use, as it's a harder metal than is brass; titanium and carbide dies help solve this issue. Please note: Some of the more inexpensive ammunition is produced with steel cases, and these should not be reloaded. A small magnet will easily identify these cases, so they may be discarded.

There are two styles of primer pockets seen in centerfire cases. Boxer primed cases are the most common and are the type used here in America. They have a centrally located flash hole, through which the spark is delivered to ignite the powder charge. Berdan primed cases, in which there are two off-center flash holes to deliver the spark when the primer is crushed against an anvil in the primer, is more rare here in the

States, but are still popular in Europe. As reloaders with conventional tools, we can only use and reform Boxer primed cases. You should *never* try to resize or reuse any Berdan primed case without the very specialized tools made for these, as you will damage your conventional reloading tools. Make sure to carefully segregate any cases that may be Berdan primed, to avoid any confusion or broken gear.

Cartridge cases are constructed in two styles: straight-walled, in which the sides of the case are either parallel or very slightly tapered from bottom to mouth; and bottlenecked, in which the cartridge diameter steps down/in at what we call the shoulder, to achieve a diameter suitable for holding the bullet. There are different loading techniques for each, which we will discuss in chapters four and five. Rifle cartridges use both types of cases. The .458 Winchester Magnum, .38-55 Winchester, .45-70 Government, .444 Marlin, and .405 Winchester are some examples of straight-walled cases, while the .22-250 Remington, .30-06 Springfield, 7mm Remington Magnum, .270 Winchester, and .375 Holland & Holland Magnum are examples of bottle-necked cartridges. For pistols, most cases are straight walled. The 9mm Luger, .45 ACP, .38 Special, and .44 Remington Magnum come easily to mind. There are a few exceptions,

(Photos both pages courtesy Massaro Media Group & J.D. Fielding Photography)

Rimmed pistol and rifle cartridges. Left to right, .45 Colt, .38 Special, .30-30 WCF, .348 Winchester, .45-120 Sharps, and .500 Nitro Express.

Rimless cartridges. Left to right, .22-250 Remington, .270 Winchester, .308 Winchester, .30-06 Springfield, and .35 Whelen.

such as the bottlenecked .256 Winchester and the .357 SIG.

Among the different cases available, there are different types of rims. The cartridge rim is located at the base of the cartridge; the primer is located centrally within it. The rim serves as the portion of the case that's grabbed by the bolt face of the pistol or rifle upon loading and is used by the extractor to extract the fired case. There are five main classifications of rims, as follows:

A rimmed cartridge is one that has a rim that extends beyond the diameter of the case body (bet you never saw that coming!). This extended rim serves to hold the case in the chamber. It also serves as a positive depth guide for headspacing. The earliest cartridge designs were rimmed, designed for single-shot and early lever-action rifles, as well as the first revolvers. Some rimmed cartridge examples are the venerable .30-30 WCF, the .357 Magnum, the .303 British, .32 Winchester Special, and .45-70 Government.

A rimless cartridge, despite its moniker, actually has a rim, but it's the same diameter as the case body, with a groove machined into the area

Rebated rim cartridges. Left to right, .270 WSM, .300 WSM, .284 Winchester, .300 Remington Ultra Magnum, and .500 Jeffrey.

just in front of the case head. Rimless cases headspace on either the cartridge shoulder (for a bottle-necked case) or the case mouth (for some straight-walled case). The firearm's extractor grabs the case by the groove in front of the case head. This design greatly facilitates cartridge feeding from a spring-loaded magazine. These cartridges saw the light of day in the late 1880s. Some examples of rimless cases are the .308 Winchester, .30-06 Springfield, 5.56mm NATO, .45 ACP, .40 S&W, 7x57mm Mauser, and .25-06 Remington.

Possibly the rarest type, a semi-rimmed cartridge has a very small amount of rim extending past the diameter of the case body, but not nearly as much as a rimmed case. It was designed for the positive headspacing capability of the rimmed cartridge, while coming close to achieving the ease of feeding from a magazine that the rimless cartridges possess. Examples of semi rimmed cases are the .25 ACP and the .444 Marlin.

A rebated rim case is one that uses a rim dimension smaller than the diameter of the case body, but this rim's only purpose is of one to serve extraction. This is a feature seen on the Winchester Short Magnum series and the Remington Ultra Magnum line, rounds designed to have huge case capacity for high velocities. Other examples of rebated rim cartridges are the .50 Beowulf, .500 Jeffery, and the .284 Winchester.

The belted magnum case, dating back to 1910, has a "belt" of raised brass ahead of the extractor groove, yet has a case head designed similarly to that of rimless cases. The theory behind this design was to provide the easy feeding from a rifle's box magazine (*a lá* rimless), while offer-ing the positive headspacing from the rim, rather than the shoulder (a lá rimmed). The British firm of Holland & Holland first offered this case design in its .375 Velopex (which never caught on) and used it again, in 1912, in its .375 Belted Rimless Nitro Express (better known as our African classic, the .375 H&H Magnum). This case led to the development of the Super .30, or .300 Holland & Holland Magnum, in 1925, and it was this belted case design that would be the basis for nearly every case that had "Magnum" in its name, includ-ing those in the Weatherby line, until the Winchester Short Magnums and

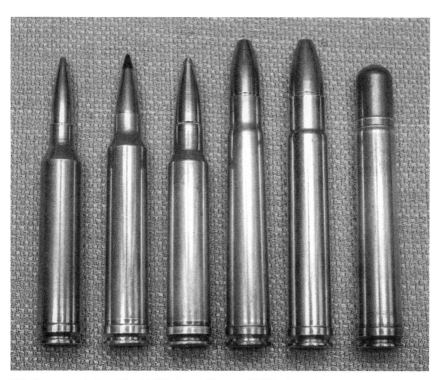

Belted magnums. Left to right, .264 Winchester Magnum, .300 Winchester Magnum, .338 Winchester Magnum, .375 H&H Magnum, .416 Remington Magnum, and .458 Winchester Magnum.

Remington Ultra Magnums came along at the turn of the twenty-first century. These newer Magnum cases are primarily based on the beltless .404 Jeffery.

CARTRIDGE NOMENCLATURE: WHAT'S IN A NAME?

Perusing through Grumpy Pants' (henceforth known as GP) hunting magazines when I was a young man, I would read about the various cartridges the authors used and be consumed. It was like finding the secret words to a magic spell—.30-30 WCF, 7x57 Mauser, .375 Holland & Holland Belted Rimless Magnum, .250-3000 Savage, .44-40, 7mm-08 Remington, .264 Winchester Magnum. The names captivated me. However, part of the mystique was born of my own ignorance. I just couldn't make sense of where the names came from nor what they stood for. An evening spent with my dad and a reloading manual (a 1970 Sierra edition that I cherish and he still uses), demystified the jumbles of numbers. If you already have a good handle on it, bear with me. If you don't, please allow me to explain.

The development of metallic cartridges required a different means of naming the particular case that the rifle used, as there were many different cases that used the same bore diameter. An early and still common example is the .45-70, often referred to as the .45-70 Government. The original designation for this cartridge was the .45-70-405. It works like this: ".45" is the bore diameter (actually 0.458-inch); the "70" is the weight of the black-powder charge (70 grains); and the "405" is the weight of the projectile (a 405-grain bullet). Many cartridges existed using this method nomenclature. Indeed, a few are still hanging around today. In 1895, the .30-30 WCF was Winchester's proprietary baby. The WCF stands for "Winchester Center Fire," where the .30 is the bore diameter (0.308-inch), and the powder charge was 30 grains of blackpowder. The .38-55 works the same way: a .38 bore (actually 0.375-inch, to be picky), with a 55-grain powder charge.

As blackpowder stepped off stage to let smokeless powder into the spotlight, the labeling changed. Peter Paul Mauser developed the 7x57mm, known better to the sporting world as the 7mm Mauser, 7x57mm Mauser, and even the .275 Rigby. The cartridge uses a 7mm bore diameter (measuring the rifle's lands; the groove diameter is 7.24mm or 0.284-inch), and the case length is 57.0mm. This led the way for naming most of the cartridges from the European Continent. The 6.5x54mm Mannlicher-Schoenauer, the 8x57mm Mauser, the 9.3x74R (the "R" stands for rimmed), and the 6.5x55mm Swedish Mauser are all examples of the metric "Continental" designation. Some included the name of the proprietor or inventor, others did not.

Sportsmen in Great Britain and America would have none of that metric nonsense. It was decimal portions of an inch for those in the UK and the USA or nothing. This

A Lapua 9.3x62mm case head.

honestly makes no sense to me, as it sort of blends different systems of measurements, but who am I to question it? The divide was so pronounced that, when the firm of John Rigby & Co. started to distribute the 7x57mm Mauser cartridge in its sporting rifles, it deemed a name change was in order, and so we have the .275 Rigby—but even that's not as simple as it may seem.

Most British cartridges (but certainly not all, as I will illustrate), are named for the diameter between the lands of the bore's rifling, not the grooves as we Americans do. The bullet (and therefore groove) diameter of the 7x57 is 0.284-inch. The land diameter is 0.275-inch and, so, the .275 Rigby was born.

Now, just when you think you may have it all figured out, you need to know that many of the British

cases use a bullet diameter larger than the name suggests. The .303 British, for instance, uses a bullet of 0.311-inch diameter, the .318 Westley-Richards uses a bullet diameter of 0.330-inch, the .404 Jeffrey uses 0.423-inch bullet, and the .500 Jeffrey uses a 0.510-inch bullet, just to name a few.

Clear as mud, right? Then it shouldn't come as any surprise that there are exceptions to all the naming rules. The most glaring example is the famous .375 H&H (short for the firm of Holland & Holland) Magnum. Its bore diameter is exactly 0.375-inch and that is the diameter of the bullets used. The popular .416 Rigby also fits this bill, with a bullet diameter that is exactly 0.416-inch. These exceptions are why you need to read your reloading manual thoroughly for each cartridge you intend to load. An assumption could be catastrophic!

The Norwegian .30-40 Krag was adopted by the US Government in 1894, using a 220-grain bullet and 40 grains of nitrocellulose (smokeless) powder. It is one of the few cases to use smokeless powder, but be named in the style of the blackpowder cartridges. Next came the case voted "most likely to succeed" by the very universe itself: the .30-06 Springfield. Based on the naming system I've just discussed, you're probably going to tell me that the name means .30-caliber with 06 grains of powder. Nope. This is just another wrench in the works. The U.S. Army designation was "Ball Ammunition, .30-caliber, Model of 1906." Somehow the name was shortened to the .30-06.

My fellow Americans tended to be a bit more creative with the naming process, sometimes rounding off the bore diameter, other times actually using a false one to differentiate the numerous cases for one bore size. Some examples of this are easy to pick up on. One of our most popular bore sizes in America is the great .30-caliber, or 0.308-inch. Many cases use this size bullet but go by different monikers. The .308 Winchester, .300 Savage, .308 Norma Magnum, .300 Holland & Holland, .307 Winchester, .30-40 Krag, .30-06 Springfield, .300 Winchester Magnum, .300 Weatherby Magnum, .309 JDJ, and .300 Remington Ultra Magnum all use the 0.308-inch bullet diameter, but the cases are in no way interchangeable.

Sometimes, metric designations are converted to English units for a new name. The 7x57 Mauser, 7mm Remington Magnum, .284 Winchester, and .280 Remington all use 0.284-inch bullets. The .280 Remington was even renamed the 7mm Express Remington for a while, to further complicate matters!

Because of the wide array of .22-caliber centerfire cartridges available, the number or caliber portion of a cartridge name is often adjusted so as to differentiate one from another. Within the selection of cases that use 0.224-inch bullets, for instance, we have the .218 Bee, .219 Zipper, .220 Swift, .221 Fireball, .222 Remington, .223 Remington, .224 Weatherby, and the .225 Winchester! Woof!

Sometimes the company that developed the case gets its name involved, such as with the .270 Winchester, 6mm Remington, or .300 Weatherby. Other times it's the last name of the developer or a tribute to the developer. The .35 Whelen is named for famed gun writer and cartridge developer Col. Townsend Whelen, and the .257 Roberts (known often as the "Bob") is a tip-o'-the-hat to developer Ned Roberts.

Then there are the times the case name comes from the combination of an existing case changed to hold a bullet diameter different than that of the original. These cases began life as "wildcats." Here in America, when we name a wildcat cartridge, the new bullet diameter is listed first, then the parent case is referenced. The .25-06 Remington is one: it is a .30-06 case resized to hold 0.257-inch bullets.

A Lapua
.22-250
case head.

The .22-250 Remington is a .250-3000 Savage case necked down to hold 0.224-inch bullets. Seems easy enough, but this method of naming gets a bit strange now and then, as in the case of the 7mm-08. This is a .308 Winchester case necked down to hold 7mm projectiles. I believe the proper terminology would have been 7mm-308, but that's not how it happened. In Great Britain, it works in the opposite manner. Instead of putting the bore diameter in front of the parent case, the parent case bore diameter is placed in front of the new bullet size. The classic .450/400 Nitro Express is a .450 NE resized to hold a 0.405-inch bullet, and the .577/450 Martini-Henry is a .577 Snider case necked down to hold 0.455-inch bullets.

Then there's the stuff that can only be called weird. Savage introduced the .250-3000 Savage, in 1915. Using light-for-caliber 87-grain bullets, it was the first cartridge to break the 3,000 feet per second (fps) mark. This was so important to the Savage Arms Company that it included the figure in the case name: A .250-diameter bullet—okay, technically it's 0.257-inch, because all of this isn't confusing enough—exceeding 3,000 fps.

However you slice it, fascinating to bewildering a general familiarity with the naming of cartridges is important to avoid a possible confusion when loading and/or shooting. I now return you to your regularly scheduled programming.

*Vintage
Winchester
No. 4 primers.*

THE PRIMER

That tiny metal cup in the center of your cartridge case head, struck by the firing pin, is the first spark in the chain of combustion that leads to a bullet being launched. The spark is created by the reaction of lead, barium nitrate, and other chemical compounds being crushed against the anvil located within the primer cup. This explosion sends sparks through the primer's flash hole and into the powder charge. The design is really just an upgrade on the first percussion caps used in the muzzleloading rifles of the mid-nineteenth century; the percussion cap, too, needed to be struck against an anvil, in this case the nipple on the percussion lock. So, the modern configuration of primers for centerfire cartridges features an anvil self-contained within the primer itself.

As a side note to the discussion on primers, know that care must be taken when firing old (WWII-era or earlier) military ammunition. Years ago, the priming compound contained fulminate of mercury, which is a corrosive substance. While commercial sporting ammunition made the switch to non-mercuric primers around the turn of the twentieth century, the U.S. military did not make the official switch until after the Second World War. If you find such ammunition and your preliminary inspection shows it to be in sound, fireable condition, be sure and clean your rifle with a good solvent after shooting it. When my pal Hicksy bought "Autumn," his sweetheart .30-06, we had a surplus of WWII military

Primer varieties.
(Photos both pages courtesy
Massaro Media Group & J.D.
Fielding Photography)

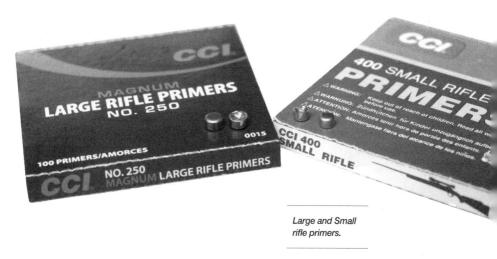

*Large and Small
rifle primers.*

Benchrest
primers.

ammunition, which we used for practice and sighting in. After taking the rifle to the range one day, he neglected to clean it until several days late—he could barely fit a patch down the bore because of the corrosion caused by those old primers. That was the last time we shot that old ammo without cleaning immediately! Thankfully, today's primers are non-corrosive.

There are two types of primers, for our purposes, in the discussion of reloading metallic cartridges: Rifle primers and Pistol primers. Each variety comes in Large and Small sizes, just as each size has a Magnum variation that has a hotter spark. Rifle primers have a thicker metal cup, due to the higher pressures at which they operate. Pistols operate at much lower pressures and, so, the primer cups are thinner. Large Rifle and

Large Pistol primers are 0.210-inch in diameter, while Small Rifle and Small Pistol primers are 0.175-inch in diameter. I've heard the myth of a "medium" primer measuring 0.204-inch, made by the Frankfort Arsenal in Pennsylvania, but I've never seen one with my own eyes.

Primer designations can be confusing, so you must make a habit of checking and double-checking your reloading data manual, so you have the correct primers for the cartridges you're loading. Here are some examples of primer nomenclature:

- Large Rifle: CCI 200, Federal 210, Remington 9½, Winchester WLR
- Large Rifle Magnum: CCI 250, Federal 215, Remington 9½ M, Winchester WLRM

CCI

100

No. 41
PRIMERS

For 5.56mm Ammunition

⚠ **WARNING:** Keep out of reach of children. See all warnings on back panel.
⚠ **WARNING:** Zündhütchen für Kinder unzugänglich aufbewahren.
⚠ **ATTENTION:** Amorces tenir hors de portée des enfants.
⚠ **ATENCIÓN:** Mantengase fiera del alcance de los niños.

CCI primers designed for military rifles.

- Small Rifle: CCI 400, Federal 205, Remington 6½, Winchester WSR
- Small Rifle Magnum: CCI 450, Federal 250M, Remington 7½
- Large Pistol: CCI 300, Federal 150, Remington 2½, Winchester WLP
- Large Pistol Magnum: CCI 350, Federal 155, Winchester WLPM
- Small Pistol: CCI 500, Federal 100, Remington 1½, Winchester WSP
- Small Pistol Magnum: CCI 550, Federal 200, Remington 5½, Winchester WSPM

There are several varieties of "Match" primers available. These have been shown to give the most consistent results and are readily embraced by the target shooting community. Several companies also produce "military primers," which have the thickest cups. These are designed for use in the AR platform and other military-type rifles and are made to military specifications. The CCI 34 (Large Rifle) and CCI 41 (Small Rifle) are two examples. These primers are designed to avoid a slam fire, something infrequently associated with the protruding firing pins of military firearms.

Always use the type *and* brand of primer called for in the reloading manual you are referring to for load data, as a change in primers can result in a change in pressure. Never substitute. It is also a good idea to have only one type of primer brand and size on your reloading bench at one time, to avoid any confusion and a possibly dangerous situation at the bench.

Different powder canisters.

THE POWDER

Warm apple pie, evergreens in November, puppy's breath, my wife's perfume—these are among my favorite scents. All of them pale in comparison to the wonderful, acrid scent of burnt gunpowder. You either know what I'm talking about or you don't.

So what is that magic stuff? What is that mystical dust that makes the sound of a tiny maraca when you shake your favorite cartridge? Some shooters never need or want to answer this question, but, being the curious human I am, I had to know. Hours in my youth spent thumbing through my dad's reloading manual admittedly left me more confused than enlightened, but that's reversed now, so allow me to shed a little light on this wonderful substance.

Friar Roger Bacon was the first European to record the mixture for gunpowder in the thirteenth century, although it is a widely held belief that Chinese culture had it long before that. Regardless, that blissful blend of sulphur, charcoal, and saltpeter called "blackpowder" certainly changed the world. It ruined the effectiveness of metal armor, diminished the security of the castle, and leveled the playing field between strong, brave soldiers and their more diminutive and cowardly counterparts.

Blackpowder hasn't really changed in its makeup over the last century and is still going strong. However, it burns dirty and leaves a corrosive residue throughout the firearm's bore that must be removed quickly to prevent rusting and pitting. Today there are cleaner burning substitutes available that have made the job of cleanup easier. Hodgdon's Pyrodex and 777 are among these. Blackpowder is generally measured by volume, not weight, and its substitutes are also measured this way. Blackpowder is graded and identified by the coarseness or fineness of the granules; Fg is very coarse cannon and shotgun powder, FFg and FFFg are finer and used in many rifles and pistols, and the finest, FFFFg, is usually reserved for priming flintlock actions.

Progress was made in the scientific field of powder in the 1840s, when nitric acid was put upon cellulose to produce nitrocellulose.

This was known as "guncotton." It was capable of producing pressures and velocities much greater than its blackpowder counterpart, and it took a bit to develop gun steel that could withstand those higher pressures. Later, in 1887, Alfred Nobel invented nitroglycerine. When mixed with nitrocellulose, it created a plasticized substance that was a stable compound. Cordite, an early British version, was the propellant *du jour* for many of our classic cartridges. One of Cordite's little peculiarities was the fact that it was very sensitive to temperature fluctuation. The cartridges that were developed in England

Flake powder grain structure.

(Photos both pages courtesy Massaro Media Group & J.D. Fielding Photography)

Stick powder.

and Continental Europe often had pressure increases, when brought to Africa and India. The Tropics showed the flaws, from extraction troubles to cracked receivers, and this is why some of the huge cases like the .416 Rigby and the .470 Nitro Express came about. They needed that kind of internal case volume to keep the pressures low.

Our modern single-base and double-base smokeless powders have resolved that issue, and the issue of temperature sensitivity has been diminished greatly. Single-base powders are usually comprised mostly of nitrocellulose; double-base powders are a mixture of nitrocellulose and nitroglycerine. Powders are coated with a deterrent and a stabilizer. The deterrent slows the burn rate to a desired amount, and the stabilizer

slows down the decomposition of the compound.

The shape of the powder granules is usually one of three types: flake, stick, and spherical. Flake powder is usually shaped like miniature pancakes. Many shotgun and pistol powders are in this configuration, and some contain colored flakes. Alliant's Green-Dot, Bullseye, and Unique are three examples of flake powder.

Stick powder is one of the most popular rifle powder shapes. The compound is extruded into long, spaghetti-like rods, then cut to the desired length. Examples of stick powder include IMR4064, IMR4350, Hodgdon's Varget and H4831, and Alliant's Reloder 25.

Spherical powder is just what you think it would be, a round ball, or at least a slightly flattened round ball.

These take up less space than stick powder and can help achieve good velocity in a case with limited capacity. Some of the spherical powders include Hodgdon's H380 and BL-C(2), Winchester's 760, and Accurate Powder's No. 9.

Powder is measured in grains, not to be confused with grams. There are 7,000 grains to the pound. Depending on the cartridge being loaded (and especially pistol cartridges) a variation of as little as a tenth of a grain can make the difference between a safely loaded cartridge and a dangerous one that produces excessive pressures. It is *imperative* that you strictly adhere to the load data published by reputable manufacturers! I cannot stress that point enough. The various reloading manuals are

products of months and years of pressure testing under strict laboratory conditions, and an attempt to exceed the published values can result in your untimely demise. Start at the published minimum charge weight and carefully increase the charge as you shoot through your loads. Always stop when you see the first signs of excessive pressure (bulged cases, blown primers, cases that won't extract, etc).

The powders available to the handloader are referred to as "canister grade" powder. They are each unique in their burn rates. Fast-burning powders are (generally) used in shotshells, small case rifle cartridges, and many of the pistol cartridges. The medium-burn cartridges work well in standard rifle cartridges and some of

Hodgdon's H335 spherical powder.

the bigger magnums. The newly developed slow-burning powders really shine in the huge overbore cases. The velocity kings like the .30-378 Weatherby, 7mm STW, .338 Remington Ultra Magnum, and .270 Winchester Short Magnum all develop their high speeds from very slow burning powders, which develop the high pressure necessary to push their bullets as fast as they do.

Today's powders go by many different names. Some are just names, like Bullseye, TiteGroup, Varget, Red Dot or Unique. Others are just numbers, such as Accurate Arms' No. 5 and Winchester's 760 and 748. Some are a combination, such as IMR7828, H380, N160, Reloder 15, etc. It is important that you are pretty well versed in the different powders, so as to avoid confusion and possible injury. An example: There are three different powders, from three different manufacturers, that contain "4350" in their names: IMR4350 ("IMR" stands for Improved Military Rifle), H4350 (Hodgdon) and AA4350 (Accurate Arms). All have slightly different burn rates and are *not* interchangeable. Strict attention must be paid to ensure that you have the powder in hand that the reloading manual specifies. This rule must be followed.

Storing powder is not a big deal, but common sense should prevail. It should be stored in a cool place, with no risk of exposure to open flames and stashed far away from children. I store my powder in a wooden box, clearly labeled, with a lockable lid. You never want to store powder in a container that will contain pressure; in the event of a fire, powder that is not under pressure will burn rapidly, but, put it under pressure and you've made a bomb. Always store powder in

Alliant Reloder 25 is a very slow-burning powder designed for magnum cartridges.

The very versatile IMR4064 powder.

(Photo courtesy Massaro Media Group & J.D. Fielding Photography)

Some powders can be used in many different applications. For example, I use Unique and TiteGroup in many different pistol cartridges, from 9mm Luger to .45 Long Colt. Now, the .308 Winchester rifle cartridge is the first round I learned to reload. My dad, GP, insisted that a 165-grain bullet on top of IMR4064 was the only way to go, and anything else was near blasphemy. In his world, at that time, there was no other powder (or cartridge, for that matter). I have used IMR4064 (because we had a ton of it) in .22-250 Remington, .243 Winchester, 6.5x55 Swedish, .270 Winchester, 7x57 Mauser, .308 Winchester, .30-06 Springfield, .300 Winchester Magnum, .375 H&H Magnum, and my sweetheart .416 Remington Magnum. This doesn't mean that this is the only powder that will work, nor the best powder in each of those cartridges. It just means that it is a powder that has a wide range of applications.

Conversely, a single cartridge may be served well by a large number of different powders. The venerable .30-06 Springfield, that classic of classics, can be fed a wide range of powders with a wide range of burn rates and provide great results across the board. For example, depending upon bullet weight, the following powders are well suited for use in the .30-06: IMR3031, IMR4064, IMR4320, IMR4350, IMR4895, and IMR 7828; Hodgdon Varget, H414, H380, H4350, and BL-C(2); Alliant Reloder 15, Reloder 17, Reloder 19, Reloder 22, Reloder 25, and 4000-MR; Winchester 748, and 760—you

its original canister and never try to relabel another container. I mark the date of purchase and the date I opened the canister, so as to use the powder in the order in which it was purchased.

Choosing a powder can be time consuming. Reloading manuals offer several selections per cartridge/bullet combination and will sometimes highlight or recommend the powder that worked best in *their* test rifle or pistol. Every barrel is different, and while the most accurate load in the manual may work perfectly fine in your firearm, sometimes you need to experiment. Too, you will inevitably end up owning more than one manual, but start with just one.

get the idea. It may take trying several types of powder before you find the accuracy you so desire.

THE BULLET

From the earliest days of firearms, where the smooth lead ball was the only projectile available up though the Civil War era of the Minié ball and on to today's super-premium, secant ogive match bullets, the bullet and *only* the bullet is what touches our game or target. Therefore, it deserves a great deal of attention.

In that little dust-up of the mid-1770s, the British Army was outshot by Revolutionaries who had firearms with rifling. The Brits, of course, had smoothbore muskets. Our soon-to-be Americans had embraced the idea that spinning the projectile made it easier to hit distant targets; the smoothbore Brown Bess muskets often threw lead knuckle balls. Later in ballistic history, the concept of the elongated bullet took accuracy to yet another level. Long, heavy-for-caliber, cast lead bullets accompanied frontiersmen across our continent.

A lineup of many different rifle bullet types.

Buffalo hunters made their living with them.

In the 1880s, as smokeless powder evolved and pushed rifle velocities to the region of 2,200 fps or so, the cast lead bullet had some trouble handling the pressures. Major Eduard Rubin, of Switzerland, had the bright idea to put a harder gilding metal (copper) on the outside of the bullet, for it to better take to the rifling and provide better accuracy at these new, previously unimagined speeds—behold, our modern cup and core bullet was born! The concept of a copper jacket filled with a lead core is still the most popular today, a design most often seen in the common soft-point bullet so many of us use.

There are many types and classifications of bullets today for rifles and

The round ball, the first projectile.

(Photos both pages courtesy Massaro Media Group & J.D. Fielding Photography)

The classic round-nose bullet.

Hornady's 170-grain flat-points were designed for the .30-30 WCF.

tols. As you peruse a bullet catalog, you will see nomenclature like round-nose, flat-nose, spitzer, spitzer boat-tail, hollowpoint, full metal jacket, and more. Really, the list goes on and on. Let's take a look at some of them.

A round-nose bullet has, you guessed it, a rounded nose or "meplat" (meplat is a fancy word for the front or nose portion of any bullet). These bullets usually have quite a bit of exposed lead at the nose, to provide good expansion, and are generally employed for use at shorter distances.

A flat-nose bullet will have a blunt nose. The rifle variety of these bullets was designed for the tube magazine of many lever-action rifles. The flat-nose concept came about to ensure that the nose of one bullet couldn't pierce the primer of the cartridge in front of it in the tubular magazine of lever-actions during recoil from a fired round, something that can set off a chain-fire reaction. Today, many pistol bullets are flat-tipped ,to provide a improved frontal diameter to better transmit energy at the target.

A spitzer is a severely pointed bullet, one whose name is a derivative of the German word *spitzgeschoss*, which roughly translates to "pointy bullet." The pointed end of the bullet allows it to slice through the air better, resist slowing down and, therefore, have a flatter, better trajectory (we're going to discuss all the physics in just a moment).

A pointed bullet whose base has been angled is called a spitzer boat-tail. The angled base improves aerodynamics, so they resist air drag even more than a regular spitzer.

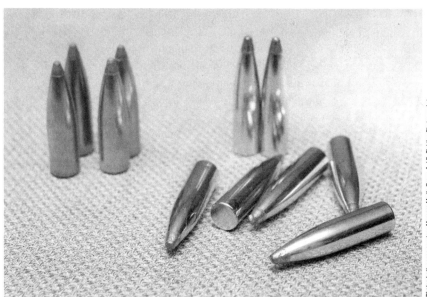

Traditional flat-based spitzer bullets.

The boat-tail on a these bullets helps reduce air drag.

(Photos this page courtesy Massaro Media Group & J.D. Fielding Photography)

Most long-range match bullets for rifle competition or other distance applications are some form of spitzer boat-tail, be they hollowpoint or otherwise.

A bullet that has no exposed lead at the nose is one that's considered to have a full metal jacket. The copper casing completely surrounds the bullet, except at the base. Military rifle and pistol bullets are mostly of this type (due to the Hague Convention).

Full metal jacket pistol bullets.

Many indoor pistol ranges require a bullet to be totally encapsulated in copper, so as to minimize the amount of vaporized lead in the air.

A bullet with a hollow cavity at the nose is, aptly, a hollowpoint, and it's a design created to rapidly expand upon striking its target. In a rifle, spitzer hollowpoint bullets can be wonderfully accurate (although their fragile construction often precludes them from being used for hunting), and can provide the target shooter with some of the best results. In a pistol, the hollowpoint configuration is often used for its terminal performance as warranted in defensive situations.

A pistol bullet that is a squared slug and without a taper to the nose is called a "wadcutter." The name is derived from the wad the bullet cuts out of a paper target.

A close cousin to the wadcutter is the semi-wadcutter. This pistol bullet has the rear portion of the wadcutter design, but a nose section tapered slightly to assist in feeding from a magazine.

Now that we have a handle on the primary bullet styles, let's discuss bullet weight. Within any one caliber (which, simply stated, is the diameter of the grooves in the barrel), there is always a range of bullet weights to choose from. Let's use the classic .308-inch diameter bullet as an example. Common .308 bullets range from 110 grains at the lightest to 250 grains at the heaviest. Since the diameter of the bullet must remain a constant, it is, therefore, the length of the bullet that must change. Within caliber, the heavier the bullet the longer it will be. This is described in the industry as "sectional density." Sectional density

A full metal jacket (FMJ) rifle bullet, shown sectioned.

is defined as the ratio of a bullet's mass to its cross-sectional area (i.e., its caliber). The higher the SD, the longer the bullet is. This is important to hunters who want to be sure

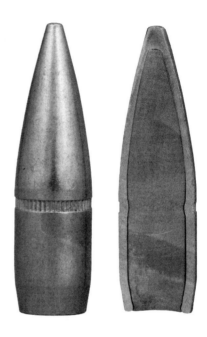

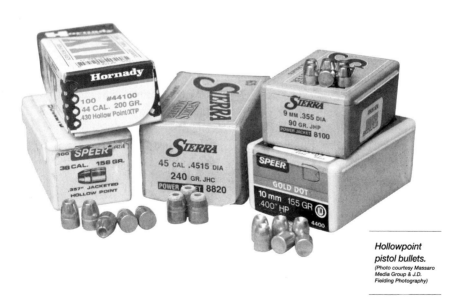

Hollowpoint pistol bullets.
(Photo courtesy Massaro Media Group & J.D. Fielding Photography)

These are .357-inch diameter 148-grain wadcutters.

their bullet will be heavy enough to match the game being pursued, so as to penetrate and make a quick kill. It is important to target shooters who want to be sure the bullets will stabilize (rotate) properly for an accurate, long-range shot.

A brief explanation of the physical effects on the fired bullet and how those effects can be controlled through bullet choice is needed here. Once fired and out the end of the barrel, the bullet immediately stops gaining velocity and begins to drop at the same rate it would if you held it in your hand and dropped it to the ground. That is known as "gravitational acceleration." The faster the object is traveling, the further it can go before contacting the earth; imagine a small child throwing a baseball versus a Major League pitcher. When a cartridge is described as being "flat

shooting," it is usually achieving higher than standard velocities. The bullet of such a cartridge will "shoot flat," because it can cover more distance before the gravitational pull of the earth has inflicted its full effect.

Now, there is more than the force of gravity at work on that poor bullet once it's sent downrange. The meplat or nose design of a bullet has quite an affect on the downrange performance of that bullet. Air drag is an awful thing. The more surface area we try to push downrange, the greater effect air drag has on velocity reduction. This is why spitzer boat-tail bullets have a flatter trajectory. They slice through the air more efficiently and resist the effects of air drag, thereby covering more ground before nasty old gravity does its thing. A round-nose or flat-nose bullet has more surface area for the

These are 158-grain .357-inch semi-wadcutters.

(Photos both pages courtesy Massaro Media Group & J.D. Fielding Photography)

air to act upon and is, thus, slowed down faster, so it cannot cover as much distance before Mr. Gravitational Pull yanks it down to the ground. For pistol cartridges, whose velocities are generally lower, this effect is minimized, plus the barrel length of pistols tends to limit them to shorter ranges, compared to the barrels of rifles.

To compare and contrast the various shapes of bullets, ballisticians developed the term "ballistic coefficient." This is the measurement of a bullet's ability to overcome air resistance in flight. The higher the ballistic coefficient, or BC, the more aerodynamic a bullet will be. If your hunting shots are all at very long ranges, a spitzer boat-tail might make an awful lot of sense. If your shooting is done at closer ranges, you'll be just fine with a round-nose or flat-nose bullet. Most rifle shooters who are serious about accuracy on paper targets prefer the hollowpoint spitzer boat-tail bullets in a "match" configuration, where the design tolerances are kept very tight.

There's been a trend in cartridge size and bullet choice that's really accelerated recently, but it's one that's really been taking place for the last 50 years. It's the concept of super-magnum rifle cartridges burning immense amounts of powder and attaining unprecedented velocities. These big cases can make long-range shooting a bit easier, because the bullets cover much more distance before the drop starts. However, they come at a price. To achieve these high velocities, we must put up

with the terrible recoil—for every action there is an equal and opposite reaction—and muzzle blast. Only you can decide where the threshold lies in a cartridge that is the perfect combination of recoil, flat trajectory, wise bullet choice, and one you can handle effectively.

I talked a bit about the basic bullet styles, but there's more to a bullet than just its external profile. In the hunting world, the construction of the bullet is very important to the quick and humane kill we all desire. The bullet must be suited to the task at hand and for the velocity at which it is delivered. Careful planning and judicious handloading can and will maximize your hunting trip and put your smiling face in the trophy picture. For those of us who pursue the most common game animal, the whitetail deer, for instance, the traditional cup-and-core soft-point bullet delivered from a classic cartridge is a perfectly suitable choice. The bullets expand well to create a large wound channel, and because the whitetail deer is a relatively thin-skinned animal, they penetrate into the vital organs to ensure a quick kill. But, not all game animal or hunting situations are the same, of course. Bears, hogs, kudus, elands, moose, and elk are just a few of the animals who have densely corded muscles or gristle plates that must be penetrated before a bullet can reach the vital organs. In the case of the largest game animals, such as moose, bison, Cape buffalo, and elephant, the animal's sheer size requires a different bullet construction, one that will not only kill the

Early premium bullets.
(Photo courtesy Massaro Media
Group & J.D. Fielding Photography)

animal, but also stop it rapidly, so that no one gets hurt. This is where the premium bullets come into play.

John Nosler was frustrated by the performance of traditional cup-and-core bullets on a large moose he hunted in the 1940s. As a result, he pioneered the development of premium bullets by adding a copper partition in the middle of the bullet, something that helped ensure deep penetration was achieved. The Nosler Partition became a mainstay in bullet designs created for hunters, and it is still used with good effect today. The Swift A-Frame took the concept one step further by chemically bonding the copper jacket to the lead core, still with the partition inside. It is a very strong bullet, capable of taking some of the largest and most dangerous game available.

Randy Brooks, of Barnes Bullets, decided that the lead core was altogether unnecessary and made a solid copper hollowpoint bullet that expanded into four petals and, so, the Barnes X bullet was born. There is

no jacket, no core, just a single piece of metal that expands and penetrates wonderfully. It has since evolved into today's TSX bullet.

Some hunters wanted the accuracy advantage of the target shooter's hollowpoint bullet, but in a configuration tough enough to effectively take game. Several companies answered this demand with the idea of a polymer tip inserted into a hollow point bullet that had a thicker jacket. The Nosler Ballistic Tip is a traditional cup-and-core hollowpoint with a sharp polymer tip and boat-tail. The Hornady Interbond and Swift Scirocco have the hollow cavity and polymer tip, but with the jacket chemically bonded to the core to prevent bullet breakup. These, among others, are wonderfully accurate bullets that can handle large game.

The hunters of the world's most dangerous game, the African elephant, often require a bullet known as a "solid." Years ago, that meant simply a bullet that had a round nose and a full metal jacket. Essentially, they were copper-clad steel with a lead core, a construct that guarantees penetration through the 2½-foot-thick honeycombed cranium of *Loxodonta Africana*. Today, that same style bullet is produced, along with a revised offering, a bullet design known as the mono-metal solid. These bullets are usually a round-nosed or flat-nosed, parallel-sided homogeneous metal, which will not deform, rivet, or break up.

On the other end of the spectrum from the elephant hunter, varmint hunters want a very accurate, yet very frangible bullet. Many bullet companies now offer a special line of bullets that have very thin jackets and are specially designed to meet the varmint hunter's needs.

Target shooters are accuracy hounds. They fine-tune their rifles and pistols and loads to produce the tightest groups possible. Such ammunition must use the finest bullets available. Since, as we shall see, consistency is the key to producing accurate handloads, the bullets for target shooters must be held to extremely tight tolerances. The match-grade bullet, with very concentric copper jackets, uniform weights, and very tight tolerances, are readily available to the target shooter, in both rifle and pistol form. Berger Bullets, with its proprietary J4 jacket, Sierra's line of MatchKing bullets, and Hornady's Match line are just a few of the projectiles available to the serious target shooter.

The cast lead bullet that started this conversation about projectiles is and will continue to be alive and well. Pistol shooters find these bullets economical, especially when high volumes of ammunition are to be expended, and they are readily available in many configurations. Rifle shooters, primarily those aficionados of the nineteenth-century lever-action and single-shot firearms, love them for their nostalgic look and performance. The cast lead bullet requires a bit more attention to load, but can produce a very satisfying finished product.

What all this talk about bullet types and design boils down to is this: Make sure the bullet you choose is appropriate for your shooting situation. If you do that, you'll have a lifetime of success and fun.

CHAPTER 3

RELOADING TOOLS

Now that you have an understanding of what a cartridge is made of, let's look at the tools you'll need to reform and assemble a cartridge. There's a long list of tools available to the reloader; some are a necessity and some simply make life easier. The setup you choose can be as simple or complex as you'd like, so long as it is effective, and by effective I mean that whether you're using all new components or brass cases that have been previously fired, you will need to be able to control the dimensions and weights of the components you are going to use.

First thing you're going to need is a clean, quiet place, one removed from distraction, in which to do your loading. A workbench with good lighting is what I prefer. Beyond that, let's look at each of the necessary tools individually.

RELOADING PRESSES

Your reloading press is the important piece of gear used to obtain a leveraged

(Photo courtesy Massaro Media Group & J.D. Fielding Photography)

The Lee Turret press that has served the author for decades.

(Photos both pages courtesy Massaro Media Group & J.D. Fielding Photography)

This is a single-stage RCBS Rockchucker.

An inexpensive Lee "C"-style press.

The strong frame of an "O"-style press.

mechanical advantage, something that's needed for resizing brass from its fired dimensions back to its original specifications, and also for properly seating a bullet in a sized case. Presses come in many shapes and sizes and are produced by a number of companies.

For most of my rifle loading work, I prefer a "single-stage" press. The single stage press performs only one operation of the various reloading steps each time the handle is worked. For me, the single-stage allows me to "feel" the resizing operation and ensures the bullets are seated the same way every time. Most single-stage presses are of the "C"-type or the "O"-type, named for the shape of their respective frame. The "C"-type

is usually more inexpensive than an "O"-type press, and they are not generally as strong, because some flex can occur under high pressure in the "C"-type designs. Since the "O"-type press can't flex, it is much stronger (and also heavier). I also like the single-stage press for the manner in which it seats the primers. This level of attention can deliver the consistent results we accuracy hounds are always yearning for.

There are also "progressive presses," which perform multiple operations every time the handle is cranked. I really like these for pistol cartridge loading. Depending on the model you choose, the cartridges are de-primed, resized, re-primed, flared, charged, and a new bullet seated, all

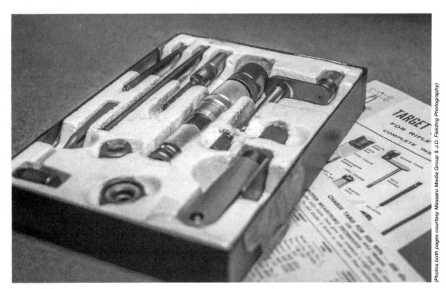

The simplest reloading setup: The Lee Target Model kit. Requires no press, just a mallet!

in a single press stroke. For the pistol shooter who likes weekend time at the range or shoots in competition, ammunition can be expended rather quickly, thus the progressive press can greatly help in replenishing supplies. In my shop, our RCBS Auto-2000 progressive press can quickly generate accurate pistol ammunition.

In addition to progressive presses, many companies offer a turret press. While still technically a single-stage by definition, the top portion of the press contains a rotating turret, which can hold three or more reloading dies at once (we'll get to dies in a minute). This turret allows the reloader to perform three or four operations without changing the dies, as you would have to do in a straight-forward single-stage press. Some folks have frowned upon the turret press, for having too much play in the turret and not holding to the tight tolerances found

in a true single-stage press. I have a Redding T7 turret press that I dearly love and I can attest to using a Lee turret press with my dad to load tens of thousands of very accurate rounds. To each their own. Whatever press you choose, make sure it is securely bolted to your bench, in a comfortable place, and that you are thoroughly familiar with its operation before you set your first case in the first die.

RELOADING DIES

Your reloading dies are the screw-in tools that reform spent brass into its proper dimensions, punch out the spent primer (the process known as "decapping"), flare the case mouth in the case of straight-walled cartridges, and seat the bullet into the case. A set of dies is specific to the cartridge you are reloading and, save for a few pistol cartridges, are not interchangeable. Reloading dies are a precisely machined image of a cartridge's specified shape within the tolerances allowed by SAAMI specifications.

So what happens with the dies? The first die you'll use is the resizing die. The press (using its mechanical advantage) squeezes the fired brass into the die and, because brass is a malleable metal, the steel (or carbide) die reforms it back into proper shape. The resizing die also has a centered

RCBS rifle reloading dies.

A dissembled seating die, with dummy round.

(Photos both pages courtesy Massaro Media Group & J.D. Fielding Photography)

An RCBS three-die set for pistol cartridge reloading.

decapping pin, used to remove the spent primer, and this pin is located below the expander ball.

The process of resizing and decapping works like this. On the upstroke of the press' ram (the ram moves up when you lower the handle of the press), the brass case is driven up into the die body and the neck or mouth portion (depending on whether it is a bottle-neck cartridge or straight-walled cartridge), is squeezed down to a dimension smaller than caliber size. On the downstroke of the ram (when you raise the press' handle back up), the case is drawn over the expander ball to open the case neck or mouth to a dimension of 0.001-inch or 0.002-inch less than the bullet diameter so that, when the bullet is seated into the reformed case, there is proper tension between the bullet "shank" (its sides) and the sidewalls of the case.

Next up is the bullet seating die. This die is used for the final step in cartridge assembly. It has a depth-adjustable cup, centered in the die, that pushes on the bullet's nose (its "ogive") when the ram is raised. This allows for precise adjustment of the seating of a bullet into the case. This die is also capable of installing a crimp of the case mouth onto the bullet, to further hold the bullet in place. Whether or not you want to put a crimp on a cartridge depends on the case you are loading and the situation at hand. Your reloading manual and the cartridge's specifications should dictate which policy is correct for your round and load. For instance, rifle cartridges that are loaded for use in tubular magazine lever-action firearms, those that are heavy recoiling, and most pistol cases often require either a roll crimp or taper crimp. Again, reading the specific cartridge requirements listed in your reloading manual and becoming thoroughly familiar with these requirements is of utmost importance. Finally, note that most bottlenecked cartridges require a two-die set: there will be one for full-length resizing and de-priming and one for bullet seating. Straight-walled cartridges require a third die that will flare the case mouth to receive the new bullet.

There is also a fourth kind of die known as a neck-sizing die. This is a special die, one usually reserved for bolt-action rounds. It resizes only the neck portion of the cartridge and is used in lieu of the full-length resizing die. The rest of the cartridge is left as a mirror of the bolt-action

rifle's chamber. The thing to know if you are going to go this route and substitute a neck-sizing die for a full-length sizing die, is that your reloaded cartridges are usable only in the bolt-action rifle from which those cases were originally fired. The bolt-action and *only* the bolt-action has the camming power to seal the chamber on a neck-sized-only cartridge. Neck-sized ammunition should never be fired in any other action type.

There are some specialty die types, such as small base dies. These are designed for resizing brass for military-style autoloaders, and they fully resize the entire length of the case body. This will ensure the cartridges feed properly from the magazine, without jams or

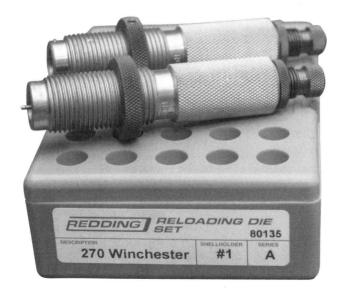

Redding dies come equipped with an Allen key for adjusting and securing the lock ring, as well as a spare decapping pin, in case the original breaks. The box can even be used as a loading block!

chambering issues.

All reloading dies come with a "lock ring," to hold the die at the depth you choose for full-length resizing and bullet seating. The lock ring butts up against the top of the reloading press. Some are held by tension alone, while others have a set screw that keeps the lock ring in place. I prefer a lock ring with a set screw, to ensure my dies will not easily come out of adjustment.

There are many different grades of reloading dies, some of the most basic construction and some made to hold very precise tolerances. Some are simple while effective, and some have deluxe features like blued steel with micrometer adjustments to allow for very precise tolerances. Like most things in life, you get what you pay for, but, with diligence, you can create very accurate ammunition with some of the more inexpensive tools. I prefer Redding and RCBS reloading dies, but use dies made by many different companies, including some that were made by companies that have long gone by the wayside and are calibrated for obsolete cartridges. As long as the dies are in good working order, you can make good ammunition with them. An occasional cleaning with a small brush and some good solvent and a light oiling should see that your dies give you a lifetime of service.

SHELLHOLDERS

Shellholders are another tool you will need. These are variously sized attachments that usually slide into the mouth of the press' ram. They are machined to hold the head of a particular cartridge and are numbered according to the size of the case head. Thus, one shellholder will often fit many different cartridges. It is very important that you have the proper shellholder for the cartridge you are loading, or you can tear off a rim or stick a case in a resizing die—not good times!

PRIMING TOOLS

There are two ways to re-prime the cartridge case, either in a handheld priming tool or in a priming device attached to a reloading press. Using

Shellholders are specifically made for a particular case head dimension.

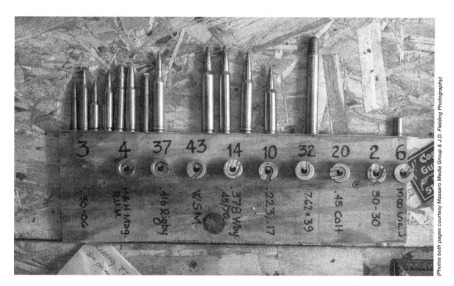

(Photos both pages courtesy Massaro Media Group & J.D. Fielding Photography)

I keep my shellholders organized on a board that is well labeled, to cut down the time spent searching for the proper one.

the handheld primer, the case is loaded into the device, a new primer inserted, and a lever is squeezed to seat the primer into the case. When the priming tool is attached to the reloading press, the primer is inserted into the priming cup and, on the up-stroke of the press handle, the primer is seated into the case.

I most often use a priming tool attached to my press. It allows for a more efficient and faster operation and I can still "feel" the primer seat to the slightly recessed level I prefer. Primer seating should be flush to the case or the little bit deeper I prefer, but you must be careful about going too deep. Your press can create a whole bunch of force, sometimes more than you need and something that will seat your primer too deep in the case. I have also used handheld priming tools to great effect. The Lyman and RCBS models in particular

have nice trays that store dozens of primers. Lee offers a simple and effective handheld primer that requires you to place one primer at a time into the hand primer. Either way and what-

A Lee handheld priming tool.

ever priming tool you choose, if you go on to become and avid reloader of multiple cartridges, sooner or later you'll need priming tools in both Large and Small primer sizes.

POWDER MEASURING TOOLS

Measuring powder is a process that requires the utmost and serious attention. An undercharge or over-charge can result in destruction and death. Nope, I'm not trying to scare you into taking up quilting instead, just being up front about what can go wrong. If you take what I say to heart, the chances of destruction (or worse) are remote at best. So, with that in mind, an accurate means of measuring powder is a *necessity*.

The traditional method for weigh-ing powder and the one I most often

Redding and RCBS beam reloading scales.

A good set of scale weights help to ensure the scale is measuring properly.

The RCBS ChargeMaster 1500 electronic scale.

employ is via the beam scale. It is capable of measuring weights down to a tenth of a grain. Gravity never wears out, and a well-calibrated beam scale will become an old friend. My RCBS 505 scale has been with me for a long time and it a great value. I also love the Redding Model No. 2 for its ultra-durable construction. I highly doubt you would wear out the hardened chrome bearing surfaces in a lifetime of loading. Whatever make or model you choose, a set of calibrating weights can help to keep things in working order.

There are also many good digital scales. They display to the nearest tenth of a grain and can be easily calibrated. But, because they work on piezo pressure, rather than true gravitational weight, digital scales tend to need to be zeroed often. I have an RCBS ChargeMaster that is among the best of the digital scales, and though I verify its reading often with a reweigh on a balance beam scale, it has yet to give me an erroneous reading. One benefit of any scale you choose is that it can also be used to weigh your bullets, should you choose to pursue a higher level of accuracy.

Should you decide to purchase a mechanical powder dispenser—there are both mechanical dispensers and hand "tricklers" that allow you to control the finest increments of a powder charge—to make the loading process quicker, the powder scale should be used to check the charge being dispensed at frequent intervals, in order to avoid a charge that is too light or too heavy. Check and check often is a good mantra no matter what measuring tools you use.

CASE TRIMMERS

Another tool you will need is a "case trimmer." Brass is malleable and, over repeated firings, will stretch or "flow." When the cartridge case becomes too long, it must be trimmed back to the proper length. It is *crucial* that the brass you intend to load be trimmed to the correct, specified length.

Trimming the brass is an important step in making good ammunition. It ensures the proper dimensions of a reloaded cartridge. Some case trimmers are a hand-cranked affair, the device bolted down to the reloading bench and carefully set to the proper measured length. Others are a machined tool of specific length and diameter, screwed into a cutting piece

An RCBS motorized trimmer.

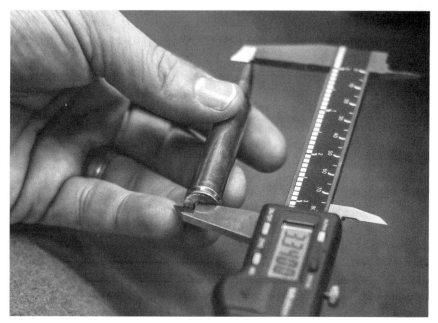

Using a micrometer to measure a completed cartridge.

and inserted into the case to then trim it to proper length. Several flicks of the wrist will do the trick. There are also some great motorized trimmers, like the RCBS Case Preparation Station, which can be fine-tuned to trim to very precise dimensions and take the wear and tear off of your hands and wrists. They cost a bit more than the hand-powered models, but, if you get the loading bug (and you will!) they save an appreciable amount of time and give wonderful results.

Being able to observe the dimensions of your resized case is necessary. A micrometer is a precise measuring tool designed to measure in inches and decimal portions of an inch. Case length, cartridge overall length (COL for short), neck diameter, and rim diameter are a few of the dimensions you will want to be able to verify.

A micrometer capable of measuring to the ten-thousandth of an inch is what you want to own. Before the digital age dawned, micrometers used a dial to represent the measurement. Today, there are plenty of micrometers with digital readouts. Some are of plastic construction and others are of metal. I prefer the metal type, as they have less room for play and maladjustment. Please don't skimp on the micrometer, you'll use it more often than you think. As your handloading techniques become more intricate, you'll rely on the micrometer more and more.

CHAMFER/DEBURRING TOOL

The chamfer/deburring tool is a little brass cutting wonder designed to remove any burrs on the inside and outside of the case mouth, while, at the same time, putting a nice, beveled edge on the inside of the case mouth. This bevel is referred to as a "chamfer." The chamfer tool has a tapering diameter, so as to be used in case mouths from .17-inch to .500-inch or bigger.

A few twists will clean up the outside of a burred case mouth easily. A clean, well-chamfered and -deburred case mouth will aid in seating the new bullet and in the chambering of a cartridge. There are handheld models that work very well, but they can give you blisters and sore wrists, if you're loading a lot at one time. Some models mount to motor-driven case prep stations and not only speed up the process, but save hand fatigue. The chamfer process is usually only necessary on bottlenecked cases, but I like to deburr all my cases, including the straight-walled rifle and pistol cartridges.

PRIMER POCKET CLEANER

The primer pocket cleaner is a steel scraping tool that removes the burnt residue left behind by the fired primer that was in residence before you decapped your case. Many of these cleaners are dual-sided, with one side for large primer pockets and the other for small. Some other models are constructed of small steel wire brushes, which will clean the pocket in a rotary action, rather than scrape the debris away. Cleaning the primer pocket will ensure that the spark of the new primer can easily reach the fresh powder charge and help to see the new primer is properly seated.

CASE CLEANING TUMBLER TOOLS

Brass is a malleable metal, yet tarnishes very easily. It must be cleaned

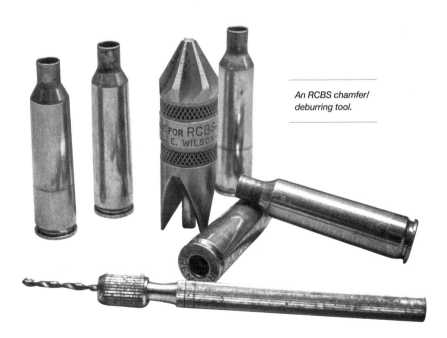

An RCBS chamfer/deburring tool.

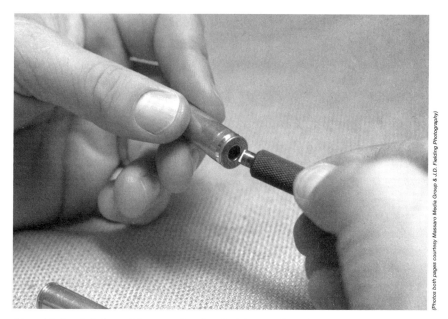

(Photos both pages courtesy Massaro Media Group & J.D. Fielding Photography)

A two-sided pocket cleaner takes care of work on both large and small primer pockets.

A Lyman Turbo 600 vibratory cleaner.

before being resized, to make sure your resizing dies give you a lifetime of good service. Using an abrasive media, such as ground corncobs or crushed walnut shells, the case tumbler vibrates a load of dirty brass in its vessel until that brass is once again shiny and clean. There are also many chemical solutions that can hasten the brass cleaning process, and I often use these in conjunction with corncob or walnut media. Tumblers come in a variety of sizes, with some capable of holding up to 1,000 pistol cases at a time. The type of reloading you intend to do should dictate the size tumbler you require.

There are ultra-sonic cleaners available, like the Lyman Turbo Sonic Cleaner, which

The ultrasonic cleaner can save time and clean your cases both inside and out.

vibrate the cases in a solution. These work much faster than traditional media tumblers. The big thing I like about cleaning ultrasonically is the way these machines clean the *inside* of the brass cases. Having the inside of the case cleaned can greatly affect the accuracy potential of your cases, in a good way, as the case volume becomes more uniform when the burnt residue from the previous firing is removed from fired cases. An added benefit to ultrasonic cleaners is that they can also be used to periodically remove the grit, brass, lube, and other accumulated dirt from your reloading dies. (You'd be shocked to see what comes out of them!) I found a chemical cleaning solution available from Iosso, which removes almost all the residue from your dirty brass. The kit comes with a cheesecloth-style pouch.

You place the dirty brass in the pouch, dunk it in the chemical cleaner for 20 to 60 seconds, and then rinse in clean water. Simple, easy, and effective, though I'd recommend a light tumbling after any chemical or ultra-sonic cleaning, to put a nice shine on your cases. Neatness counts.

CASE LUBE

Before squeezing a fired case into a reloading die, that case must be lubricated. If not, you risk having the case getting wedged in the resizing die during the process. Case lubricants come in waxes, sprays, gels, etc. Lots of options. Most gels and sprays are required if you choose to use a lube pad, a sponge-like material upon which the cases are rolled, the lube in the pad thereby evenly dispersing it-

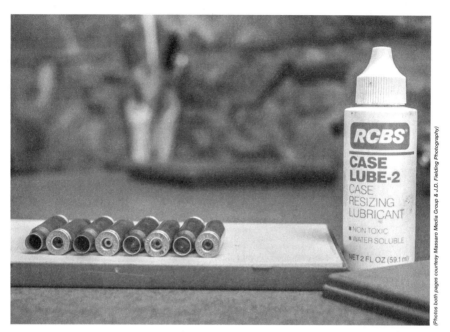

RCBS Case Lube and Lube Pad.

self on the entire case. This process of lubrication is a fickle thing. Too much lubricant and you will have hydraulic dents in the shoulder section of a bottlenecked case. Too little will result in a stuck case. I have always used the RCBS Case Lube and a lube pad. I know how much to use, and the lube comes off the cases rather easily, with just a light wiping after sizing. It will take a bit of practice and experience to judge the proper amount of lube, when you're first learning to load. Nonetheless, it is a necessary step in the resizing process.

CASE BRUSH

These little gems, of varying calibers, will help remove any excess lube or media from inside the case neck of your clean cases. They're kind of self-explanatory.

CASE LOADING BLOCKS

Case loading blocks can be a great aid. They are designed to hold the cartridges you are loading, simple as

A Tipton case brush.

that. Case blocks are a small platform or tray in which holes have been drilled or formed to a specific rim diameter, so that the cases don't fall over or roll off the reloading bench. They can be made of pre-formed plastic, or you may make your own by drilling properly sized holes into a wood block.

FLASH HOLE REAMER

The flash hole is the only means of getting the primer's flame into the powder charge. While most of today's cases are manufactured to high tolerances, sometimes small burrs or slightly out-of-round flash holes appear. A reamer or a drill bit of exact flash hole diameter (0.08-inch) can clean up the flash hole and make sure you get consistent ignition.

POWDER FUNNEL

Once the powder charge has been weighed, getting it into the case requires a funnel. I like a quality plastic funnel that resists static electricity. Such a funnel eliminates any powder clinging to the funnel walls. Most of the common funnels are dimensioned for use in cases of .22-caliber through .45-caliber, though there are specialty funnels, too. Loading the diminutive .17 Remington (as Col. Le Frogg has me load so often), requires a special funnel with a smaller hole in the end, to make sure the powder doesn't spill out around the mouth of the tiny case. If you load any of big .470s or .500s, you will need a bigger-mouthed funnel. Some cases, such as the Winchester Short Magnums and Remington

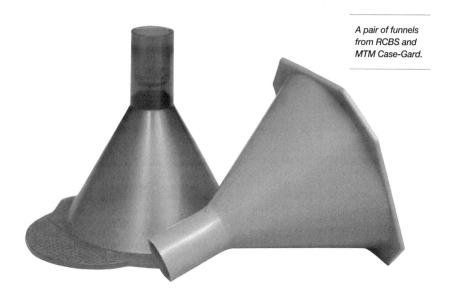

A pair of funnels from RCBS and MTM Case-Gard.

Ultra Magnums, have a very sharp shoulder and short neck, so the most common funnels available will give you headache. Because of the length of the common funnel's mouth, powder can spill around the cartridge shoulder. Years ago, after spilling powder all over the bench, GP and I customized a standard funnel we nicknamed "Stumpy," by cutting the funnel mouth length down until we had no spillage. Today, these funnels are available for purchase, properly sized for the aforementioned cases.

POWDER THROWER

A powder thrower is a dispenser of powder. It uses a large plastic vial to hold the store of powder and has a mechanism to throw a predetermined, measured amount of powder. The hand-operated variety works like this: On the up crank of the handle, the adjustable chamber is filled with powder; on the down crank, that charge is dispensed out of the lower tube and onto the pan of the scale.

The electronic age has seen the development of automated powder measurers with digital displays. The operator punches in the desired charge weight and, via an electronic motor, the machine dispenses the powder onto a digital scale until the exact amount has been poured out. I do appreciate and use the digitized devices, but I am still a fan of hand-weighed charges and beam scales.

The Redding Model No. 3 powder measure and the RCBS UniFlow powder measure are a couple of my favorite models, as they are easy to use and throw a very accurate amount of pow-

An RCBS UniFlow Powder Measure.

der. The Redding LR-1000 is designed for the shooter who loads powder charges upwards of 100 grains, and it can be a great asset to the shooter who is loading for the big safari magnums or something like the .338 Lapua. It

sure beats scooping out 100-plus grains of powder for each case!

POWDER TRICKLER

I mentioned a powder trickler before, but here's more on what this tool does. While weighing powder charges, whether you scoop the powder out or use a powder measure to throw powder onto the scale's pan, you will need to add in that last little bit to make the charge weight perfect. This is where the powder trickler comes in. Shaped a bit like an hourglass, it has a longitudinal tube threaded like a worm screw, which delivers small amounts of powder when you twist the knob. The last few tenths of a grain are precisely delivered into the pan. I have a well-worn RCBS powder trickler that has served me very well for more than 20 years.

PRIMER TRAY

Primer trays are designed to hold the primers you intend to seat in the cases. A handy tool like this eliminates the awful chore of picking up primers off the floor on hands and knees once you've dropped them. I've done it and, inevitably, you will,

A Redding LR-1000 powder measure.

(Photos both pages courtesy Massaro Media Group & J.D. Fielding Photography)

An RCBS Primer Tray.

too. There are better ways to pass the time than searching under the bench for the last three or four lost primers, so the cost of these simple trays is a worthwhile investment.

The RCBS Powder Trickler.

RELOADING MANUALS

I use the plural in this title because, sooner or later, you will need more than one. Nearly all the manufacturers of component bullets and/or powder offer a reloading manual for sale; for those produced by bullet makers, those manuals are specific to each company's bullets. The loads are developed and researched on high-tech pressure testing machines, using a variety of powders that are viable with a particular cartridge. Such data can tell you which powder performed best during the company's testing and provide you with the velocities obtained in the test rifle. Each cartridge covered usually comes with a brief history, and some will provide some helpful loading instructions.

Note that not every powder that can perform well

A good collection of reloading manuals is a must.

is tested by every company. Most often, the ballisticians choose what they feel are the powders that should perform well in a given case and test those. This can pose a problem, if you have a great quantity of a powder that you like, yet the Whiz-Bang Bullet Company's manual didn't test its new 154-grain polymer-tip-bonded-core-blessed-by-the-gods-boat-tail bullet with that powder you so love. If you have a different manual that provides load data with a comparably shaped projectile of the same exact weight, you can use the starting load and *carefully* increase the charge, looking for the first slight sign of pressure and stop-

ping your shooting immediately if it occurs. The same idea applies to older versions of annual and semi-annual manuals. They are well worth keeping around, because they can provide data for powders that are no longer produced, but that you still have a supply of (and is still safe to shoot). I have found several very accurate loads hiding within manuals that are older than I. Personally, I hoard them for their inherent value and actually enjoy reading them (this might be a touch of geekdom) for the insight they provide. They are also a valuable source of loading data for cartridges that have or will become obsolete.

When you pick a bullet and powder charge for the cartridge you intend to load, compare the test firearm data to the firearm you are loading for. The difference between the barrel length of the test gun and your gun may result in a change in the velocity you receive from the published data. I load many different types and makes of bullets, so I like to have as many of the different company manuals on hand as I can, be they in hard copy or digital form. Whether you start with just one manual that satisfies your needs for loading just one or two different calibers or you opt for several, I'll reiterate, read the manual for the cartridge/bullet combination you choose and be sure to double-check it during your loading session.

We're lucky to be reloading in the twenty-first century. In addition to the hard copy books, most companies that produce bullets and/or powder provide a wealth of reloading data on their websites. Not every bullet/case/ powder combination is tested, but the data provided can be invaluable. I often consult the information on these websites in conjunction with the printed manuals, either as an alternate source of loading data or to confirm the loads printed in the manual.

ODDS AND ENDS

While what you've just read covers the necessities, there are many additional tools that can make life on the reloading bench easier. Pliers both regular and needle nosed, screwdrivers, wrenches, Allen keys, and other common tools come in handy for adjusting presses and dies. Small brushes are great for cleaning away the little bits of brass that accumulate on the press or to clean up a spill of spent primers. Blank stickers are great for labeling your stores of brass and finished boxes of ammunition. Plastic boxes for cartridge storage and for storing tools and other accoutrement should also

(Photos both pages courtesy Massaro Media Group & J.D. Fielding Photography)

A good selection of tools always comes in handy.

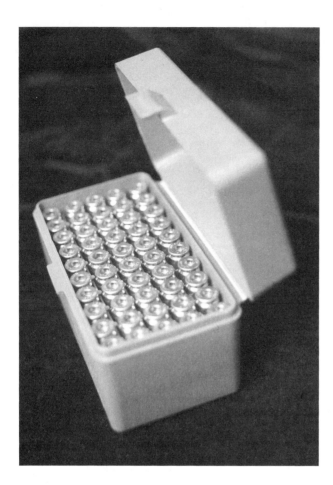

Lapua cases comfortably nestled in an MTM Case-Gard cartridge case storage box.

come in handy. Construction date, charge, bullet, etc., labeled on the cartridge box will help keep things well organized.

DATA NOTEBOOKS

A means of keeping an accurate record of your loading trials and errors, successes, and overall results is very important. I use two methods. I keep my very precious notebook, in which I describe all the load data and notes regarding each load, so that I may replicate it at any point in time, and I also keep an ".xl" file on my computer, along with a well-organized backup version of my loading data. This recorded data should include the cartridge, brand of case, number of firings through that case, the bullet make, model, and weight, the primer used, the type of powder and charge weight, and the cartridge overall length (COL). Guard your loading notes well, for they are irreplaceable and represent the only record of all your hard work.

***

Keeping accurate records is a must in reloading.

Now that we've discussed the tools for cartridge construction, let's cover the "erasers," those tools that can undo the mistakes we all make along the way.

STUCK CASE REMOVER

Sooner or later, it will happen to you. A case too lightly lubed will stick in a resizing die and, on the down stroke of the press arm, the rim of the case will rip off. This immediately ends your reloading session.

The stuck case remover can heal your woes. It is a simple tool set, but with it you can drill and tap a large hole through the flash hole and web of the case. Then, using a large screw, the tool draws the case out of the sizing die.

A quick tip for use with this tool. Be sure to back the expander ball and rod all the way out of the die, or as far as possible, so the drill bit doesn't break the decapping pin or damage the expander ball when it drills through the cartridge's web. I've forgotten to do this and broken the pin and damaged the ball to the point where I've had to order a new one. Talk about ending your reloading session. Sheesh.

BULLET PULLER

Let's say you've seated your bullet too deep in the case or, worse, forgotten to install a primer into a case in which you've charged and seated a bullet. What now, throw it away? Nope, not at all. The bullet puller erases this mistake in short order.

There are two common types of bullet pullers: The inertia-hammer and

Using the case remover to back out a stuck case.

An RCBS collet-style bullet puller.

the press-mounted model. The hammer model looks like a hammer, with a screw cap on the rear portion. An appropriate collet is placed around the cartridge rim, the cap screwed back on, and you swing the hammer down onto a block of wood. A couple swings later and the bullet pops out, along with the powder. The press-mounted model uses a collet in the same location where you would screw in a reloading die. The collet bites on the bullet and the down stroke of the press separates bullet from case. Voila! You're back in business! You may not be able to reuse the bullet, and you may need to resize the case, but it's better than wasting all the components.

CHAPTER 4

CASE WORK

Okay, folks, there you are with all these fancy reloading tools and a happy pile of spent brass on you reloading bench. Now is the time to use those tools to turn that brass into clean, shiny, reformed cases suitable for loading. Habits, be they good or bad, are easily formed, so let's form good ones. Are you ready? Let's go!

Rigorous case inspection is a must.

(Photo courtesy Massaro Media Group & J.D. Fielding Photography)

CASE INSPECTION

The first and easiest part of the program is the initial visual inspection of each case. I primarily check all the case heads, to make sure I am using and cleaning only one particular caliber at a time. It's not hard to mix up .308 Winchester with 7mm-08 Remington, a .38 Special with a .357 Magnum, a .30-30 WCF with a .32 Winchester Special, or a .25-06 Remington with a .270 Winchester, and the reloading dies sure won't like it if you screw this up. A quick glance at the inscription on the head of the cases will solve this problem.

At this point, go ahead and also inspect the cartridge head. A bent or damaged rim can cause a case to become stuck in the shell holder or, worse, jammed in a firearm. Those with damaged rims should be discarded.

Your cases will be cleaned to remove any minor surface corrosion, but any severely corroded cases should not be used. A ruptured case can be the result of loading a case that has become too thin, due to excess corrosion. The case neck can often split, either in a line parallel with the case body or perpendicular to it; sometimes, excessive pressure will cause a split in the case body. A magnifying glass and good lighting

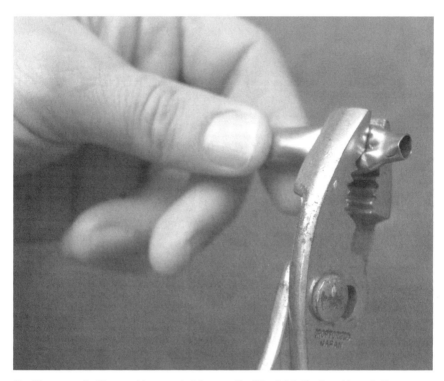

Crushing a case that is unusable prevents it from making it back into the "good brass" pile.

will reveal these slight cracks. Destroy and discard any split case. Brass cases can be reused several times, but, at the first sign of an unsafe situation, they should be destroyed and discarded. When I find cases that are unsuitable for use, I crush the case mouths closed with a pair of pliers and toss it into the metal recycle bin, so that they have no chance of being reused.

Some cases have stretched too much from repeated firings. When this happens, they develop a very bright ring near the web of the case. This ring is caused by the case metal becoming thinner in this area, and it can result in case head separation. The case can actually break in two or partially split, neither of which is

a good thing. A paper clip or other piece of similar wire, bent to a right angle at the end, can make a good "feeler-gauge." Stick the wire in the case and, if you feel a detent on the inside of the case wall in the area of the shiny ring, do not use that case any further.

CASE CLEANING

Spent cases can be not only become tarnished, but downright dirty. They often fall onto the ground after being fired and, so, collect dirt and dust. Burnt powder residue adds to the gritty mixture. Either way, cases must be cleaned to ensure they do not damage the

Once-fired cases in the tumbling media.

resizing die or feed improperly into your firearm. I use a vibratory brass cleaner, often referred to as a tumbler (some cleaners actually do tumble the brass, while others simply vibrate it among the media). The vibratory cleaner usually consists of a motor beneath a plastic tub, though sometimes it's a belt-driven tumbling chamber that resembles a small clothes dryer drum.

To use the tumbler/vibratory cleaner, cleaning media, such as ground corncobs or crushed walnut shells, is dumped into the tub, along with your dirty brass. Once the lid is in place, the vibratory or tumbling action scours the brass cases clean. A chemical cleanser, like Lyman's

Sifting out the tumbling media.

Turbo Brite and even good old Brasso, can be added to help speed up the cleaning process. A couple hours of your brass happily dancing in the whirlpool of media should have it all shiny and ready for action.

It is not uncommon for the media to become packed into the case, when they've been in the tumbler. It is absolutely necessary to be certain that all the cleaning media is removed from the cases. You can sift your brass around in an old colander, so that the media can drop through the holes and back into the tub, or a good old paper clip can be used to remove the media from the cases by hand. Either way, the cases must not have any media or other foreign substances inside them. Finally, a case brush will help to loosen any media stuck to the side of the case walls.

Ultrasonic cleaners cut the cleaning time down considerably. They use a cleaning solution, often sold as a concentrate, to clean both the inside and outside of the cases. Often the cleaning time is 10 minutes or less, and these cleaners do a very good job. I believe the ultrasonic cleaners are the wave of the future for cleaning brass. I know my Lyman 2500 model

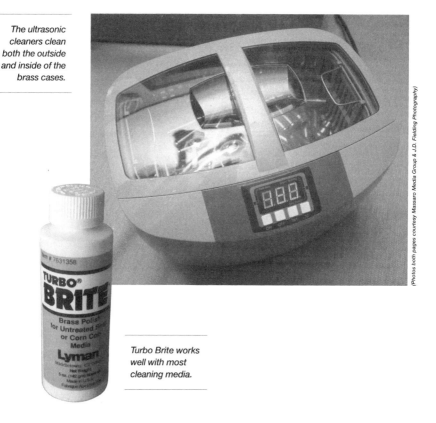

The ultrasonic cleaners clean both the outside and inside of the brass cases.

Turbo Brite works well with most cleaning media.

(Photos both pages courtesy Massaro Media Group & J.D. Fielding Photography)

Rolling the cases to be resized across a lube pad.

does a great job. I still toss the clean cases in the tumbler for a brief time once they're out of the ultrasonic, to give them a good polished shine.

Some slight tarnish marks that are not removed by the cleaning are acceptable. If you're a stickler for having things bright and clean, so be it, but I've shot some very impressive groups with brass that had my fingerprints tarnished into them. The goal is to have clean brass that is free from dirt or grit, not necessarily to have a shine good enough to win a best brass contents on the range. I usually wipe down all the cases with a clean rag and reinspect the cleaned cases as a last step before resizing.

One thing to know is that nickel-coated cases need not be tumbled. They require only a simple wiping, to be sure no grit remains on the cases. They do need to be lubricated later on though, (unless you're using carbide pistol dies).

LUBRICATION

Brass cases that are to be resized must first be lubricated, so they can be worked over the expander ball and removed from the die without sticking. The sizing die is really a forcing cone, and the press has the ability to really wedge those cases into the die if there is not enough lubricant present to enable their removal.

Lubricants for cases come in many forms. Gels, sprays, and waxes are among the most popular. I prefer the gel lubricants, like RCBS Case Lube. The gel is spread evenly onto a sponge-like lube pad and then the cartridge cases are rolled over it. Make sure the lube pad is as free from dirt and grit as possible, as such debris can transfer onto the cases and foul your resizing die. Spray lubricants come in an aerosol can and can lubricate a large number of cases simultaneously. Case wax can be rubbed onto your fingers and then applied to cases. I've even heard of some folks using car wax or shoe polish as a lubricant, but I can't verify the results. I recommend a lubricant from a reputable reloading supply company.

It will take a bit of experience to achieve the proper level of lubrication. Too much and you will hydraulically dent the cases. Too little and you will get the case stuck in the die. Don't forget to add a very small bit of lubricant to the case mouth. Also note that your resizing die may have a vent hole that allows trapped air and excess lubricant to escape during the resizing process. Make sure this hole is free from obstruction so that the die will function properly. A paper clip end seems to fit well and makes a good cleaning tool for this vent.

Dies come in steel and carbide (and some aluminum). You will most likely start out with steel, and that's the type of die most bottleneck cartridges require. For most pistol cartridges, however, tungsten carbide dies are where most reloaders tend to lean. These dies usually don't require a lubricant to resize the cases. It should be noted that carbide dies are designed to be used without the "cam-over" (which we'll talk about in the next chapter), and should be set up to just make contact with the shellholder. The carbide insert is also more brittle than traditional steel or aluminum dies, so take care not to drop them onto hard surfaces, as they may shatter. You should read the manufacturer's specifications, if you choose to use carbide dies, and follow them to the letter.

RESIZING AND DEPRIMING

It is now time to start using the press and dies, even though, at this point, you're not reloading. Rather,

A disassembled resizing die, showing the expander ball and decapping pin.

(Photos both pages courtesy Massaro Media Group & J.D. Fielding Photography)

these next steps are actually a continuation of the case preparation process.

Your press should be securely bolted to the bench and you should have the following tools assembled: reloading dies and the necessary tools to adjust them; proper shellholder for the cartridge you're reloading; case lubricant; and your pile of spent brass. I like to neatly place the brass to be resized into a loading block.

Before I install the resizing die, I unscrew the rod that holds the expander ball and decapping pin. Take the expander ball portion of the die and remove any of the rust inhibitive material used for shipping, then lightly lubricate it. Reinstall the rod and lower the decapping pin within the die body until it protrudes from the bottom portion of the resizing die somewhere between $3/16$-inch and a $1/4$-inch. This is far enough below the bottom of the die for it to reach through the case's flash hole and push out the spent primer. If the decapping pin extends any further than this, the case web may damage the expander ball during resizing. A few cartridges, such as the .22 Hornet, require a lesser amount of the decapping pin be exposed. With your decapping pin set, slide a shellholder of the proper size for your cartridge into the ram of the press, at the slot at the top of the ram.

The next step is to set up the resizing die to function properly. Be certain to read and re-read the instructions that come with your brand of reloading dies, for proper resizing adjustment. The die will have several thread-adjustable parts. The depth of the decapping pin is adjustable, as you've just seen, as is the overall depth of the die itself. To make your adjustment, the press' ram should be fully extended upward, with the shellholder inserted in place. Next, the resizing die should be screwed down until it firmly meets the shellholder. Depending on the manufacturer of the dies you chose, this may suffice for full-length resizing.

Every resizing die and press is a little different. RCBS recommends that once the ram is fully extended upward and contact is made with the shellholder, the ram is then lowered and the die screwed down another quarter-turn. This will force the press to squeeze the case fully into the die body, resulting in a full-length resizing of the shell. Redding dies require that the die body just touch

Unsightly hydraulic dents in the shoulder portion of these .308 cases show signs of using too much case lube.

Annealed Hornady brass, showing the annealing marks created during the manufacture of the new case.

the shellholder. It is very important to read the literature provided with your particular die set and follow that company's procedures to the letter.

Lower the ram all the way down and slide a lubricated case into the shellholder. Lever the press' handle down, lifting the ram and driving the case up into the die. Expect to meet some resistance as the case is returned to its original size, just as it was before firing. With the case firmly up in the die, the spent primer should now pop out of the primer pocket. Raise the press' lever and, on the down stroke of the ram, the case neck or mouth is now drawn over the die's expander ball to return it to caliber diameter.

If all went well and the die was set up properly, your case should now be resized. Still, this is your first case, and there are a few common problems that should be covered here and should be corrected.

If you're resizing a bottlenecked cartridge and, upon removal from the resizing die, you see little dents in the shoulder area of the case, you have over-lubricated the case. These dents are called "hydraulic dents," and they are a result of the lubricant having no means of escape from within the die. If the dents are not severe, they will "shoot out" upon the next loading and firing, as the case will be forced once again to expand to the size of the firearm's chamber. They are unsightly, but not necessarily dangerous, unless you are working near maximum pressures—which you should not be, as a new reloader. If you have any doubt, do not load these cases again.

Cases that have been previously fired will certainly need the resizing procedure described above, but I also give the same treatment to new brass. Often times, new cases will have dented case mouths, that damage incurred during the shipping process, so these new cases can benefit from being resized and then trimmed to a uniform overall length. Now, if you receive your new cases, especially bottlenecked rifle cases, and you notice a rainbow hue to them, especially in the region of the mouth and the neck, do not fear. This is a sign of annealing during the manufacture of the case, rather than the sign of an over-pressure load that you would see in previously fired brass. Annealing of brass is the process of rapidly heating the metal to soften it. Brass, when worked by hand, becomes brittle, yet, when heated and cooled, it becomes softer. Some companies, like Hornady, will anneal their unprimed cases to give the longest case life possible. Annealing your own brass is a tedious process and beyond the scope of this book, but do not fear the slight discoloration of good annealed new brass.

Finally, if you press a case up into the resizing die and are unable to remove it or, even worse, rip off the rim portion, you'll need some help. The removal of the stuck case is covered in a later chapter.

Okay, let's say you got through your first round of brass resizing problem free. At this stage, I reinspect the cases, looking for neck cracks and other problems. Destroy and discard any that are not satisfactory.

NECK SIZING

This process, in which only the neck portion of the case is resized, is usually reserved for reloads being used in bolt-action rifles. Neck sizing *only* works when preparing ammunition for the rifle in which it was

Neck sizing usually requires a dedicated die.

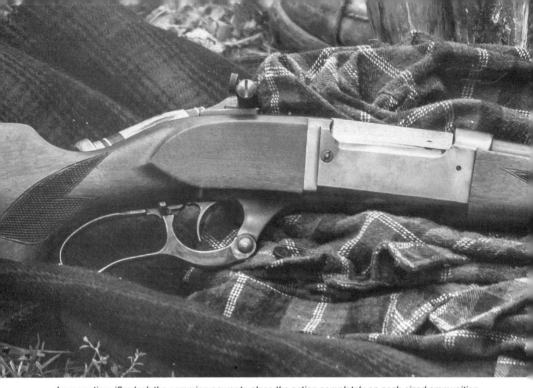

Lever-action rifles lack the camming power to close the action completely on neck-sized ammunition. The practice of neck-sizing only should be reserved for brass to be used in bolt-action rifles only, and only the rifle from which the brass was obtained in the first place.

previously fired. Because they are not fully resized, meaning the body of the case is still a perfect reflection of the chamber of the rifle it was fired in, these neck-sized cases are usable only in the rifle in which they were fired, i.e., they may not be used in any other rifle of the same chambering.

The process of neck sizing is rather simple, because only the neck area (or a portion of the neck area) of the case is resized to hold the bullet, while the shoulder and case body are left alone. The logic in this is that the case body has been custom-formed to its rifle's chamber and, so, by not resizing this portion of the case and, instead, leaving it as a "fire formed," mirror reflection of its rifle's chamber, upon chambering as a reload, that

case will provide tighter tolerances and, therefore, better accuracy.

If you are a bolt-action rifle shooter and choose to only neck resize, enough of the neck should be sized to provide good bullet tension within the case neck. A special neck-sizing die is usually used for this function, although a full-length resizing die can be backed out of the press by one turn or so to achieve a similar result. Your goal is leave the body and shoulder area alone, and it may take some experimentation with your dies to do just that (and, so, you can see why a dedicated neck-sizing die saves some of this hassle). I'd like to note once again that only bolt-action rifles have the ability to "cam" the chamber closed; slide-action, lever-action, and semi-automatic rifles do *not* have this ability. Also know that, with neck-sized ammunition, upon loading the cartridge and closing the bolt, you will probably meet more resistance than you would on a new or fully resized cartridge. That's the improved tolerances you are feeling.

When lubricating the brass for a neck-sizing die, only the neck portion of the case needs be lubricated. A properly set up neck-sizing die will not make contact with any other portion of the case.

CLEANING THE PRIMER POCKET

Now your cases are resized and their spent primers are pushed out, so it's time to pay attention to the primer pocket now that it's exposed. You should see some of the burnt residue from the fired primer in the primer pocket. With a few twists of the wrist, the primer pocket cleaner

will scrape out that residue and allow the new primer to be seated in a clean environment.

The flash hole should now be inspected to assure that no debris or cleaning media has been lodged within it. I use a small drill bit of the same diameter as the flash hole to remove any slight burrs, but make sure you don't enlarge the flash hole when you perform this task. A clean and uniform flash hole will give a constant ignition, getting us one step closer to good accuracy.

TRIMMING THE BRASS

Every cartridge has an established case length, as defined by SAAMI. Your reloading manual will tell you this measurement, and it is important to have your cases meet this value. Brass tends to flow or stretch upon firing, and the first place you will

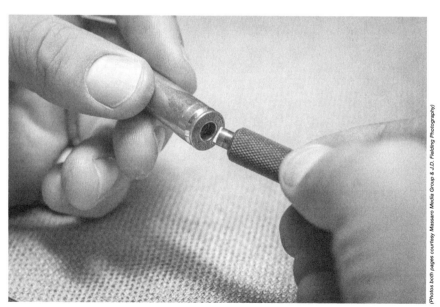

A clean primer pocket is an absolute necessity.

(Photos both pages courtesy Massaro Media Group & J.D. Fielding Photography)

notice it is in the length of the case. Your micrometer will allow you to accurately measure the cases, and any that are longer than acceptable length must be trimmed down.

A bench-mounted rotary case trimmer can be set to the desired length and the cases then trimmed down. The Lee Company makes a neat little device using a universal cutter and a

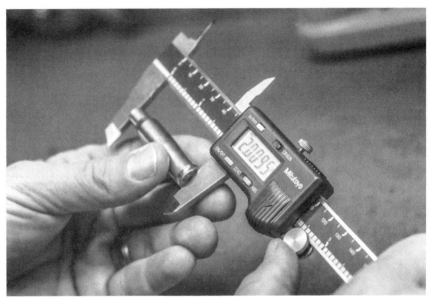

Using a micrometer to measure your trimmed brass will give the best degree of accuracy.

Lee makes a very sensible tool that quickly provides well-trimmed brass.

steel length gauge that features a pin that slides through the flash hole. The length of the steel gauge is in accordance with the SAAMI specification. The case rim is held in place by a shellholder-type clamp. You can trim by hand or insert the shellholder into a portable drill and trim your brass to the proper length. These steel gauges are cartridge specific, so you'll need one for each cartridge you intend to load. The bench-mounted trimmers, whether hand-crank or electric motor-driven, are a bit more universal in their application.

Once the cases are all trimmed to the proper length, the chamfer/deburring tool is used to smooth out the inside and outside of the case mouth. This tool cuts the brass a bit, leaving a cleanly shaped case mouth for the bullet to be seated into. Finally, the case brush is used one more time, to remove any small pieces of trimmed brass from the neck of the case.

Now, there are several newfangled gadgets that do many of these steps at once. As an example, the RCBS Case Preparation Station is a rotary, electric motor-driven tool that takes care of the trimming, primer pocket cleaning, and chamfering in one concise unit. The trimming portion is adjustable via two set screws and a micrometer and is capable of trimming the brass to very precise dimensions. The spring-loaded shellholder will hold cases of any and all case head dimensions, and the cutter face will see that all the case mouths are trimmed squarely. Then, on the top of the unit, six rotary attachments help with the remaining steps. There are stainless steel brushes in both large and small primer pocket sizes that spin away to clean the dirty primer pockets of your cases. Next, the rotating chamfer/deburring tool awaits the case mouth of your sparkly clean cases and removes any and all burrs there to ensure

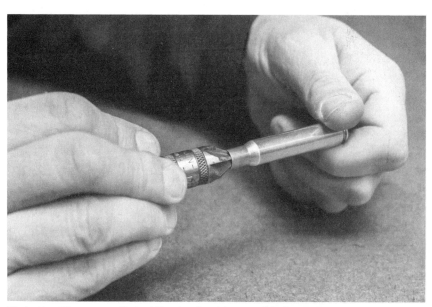

The inside of the case mouth should be chamfered, for smooth bullet seating.

Make sure there are no rough brass edges on the case mouth after trimming.

The motorized trimmer has many different caliber pilot sizes, for accurate trimming.

The rotating steel brush primer pocket cleaner.

smooth bullet seating. In a nutshell, this little device and others like it can save you many blisters and sore wrists, while producing well-trimmed and cleaned cases ready for loading.

Some loading manuals suggest that you should trim your brass to a smaller dimension than specified by SAAMI. This method allows for the stretching of your brass upon firing. If this makes sense to you, that's fine. I think there are two potential problems with this trick. In the bottlenecked cartridge, in cutting shorter than SAAMI spec, you are reducing the amount of neck tension on the bullet. In a straight-walled cartridge, this shorter trim will slightly reduce the case capacity, as you must crimp the bullet on the case mouth and the overall case

length will be reduced. Whether or not this has a dramatic effect on performance is arguable, but I always trim my brass to the SAAMI specification. Either way, I recommend you keep all your brass a single uniform dimension, so, as you develop your loads, you don't change any aspect of the finished cartridge and keep the pressures to a safe level.

FLARING THE CASE MOUTH (STRAIGHT-WALLED CASES ONLY)

Straight-walled cases must be flared at the case mouth in order to properly load a bullet into them. Loading a bullet into a straight-walled case without the proper amount of flare often results in a crumpled case. This is especially true with the full

The chamfer tool atop the RCBS Case Preparation Station.

Deburring the case mouth.

metal jacket bullets so popular with shooters using indoor ranges for pistol practice or competition. In fact, the sharp, square, rear portion of the FMJ *must* be seated into a flared case.

The flaring die is the third die included in most sets of dies for straight-walled cases. It has a slightly larger-than-caliber plug in place of the spot where the decapping pin would be, which will flare or open the mouth of the case to a bigger diameter than the bullet to be loaded. The flared case may look strange at first, kind of like a colonial blunderbuss. Rest assured, upon seating the bullet in a properly adjusted bullet seating die, the flared portion of case mouth will return to its proper dimension.

To flare a straight-wall case, adjust the flaring plug down within the die until you see the case mouth flare no more than $1/16$-inch down the case. If you flare a case too much, it cannot be returned to proper dimension in the seating die. Over-flaring also results in a diminishing of case life, as the mouth of the case is worked too much and, so, will become brittle prematurely. I flare all the cases I intend to load at one time and place them into the loading blocks for the loading process.

There's one last step to perform in your case preparation before you begin the actual reloading process. At this stage, I give the cases a good wiping with a clean rag, to remove any lubricant or brass filings that may have adhered to the case.

I would like to note that a progressive reloading press can perform

A .38 Special case before flaring.

The same .38 Special case after flaring.

From left to right, the case before flaring, the properly flared case, and an over-flared case.

A flaring plug within the flaring die.

The shellplate and frame of the RCBS Pro2000 Auto Index progressive press.

many of these operations simultaneously. Each stroke of the press' ram can perform several operations at once: resizing, depriming, flaring, priming, powder charging, bullet seating, and crimping. There are usually five different stations to a progressive press, along with a base plate that rotates the case around to each station in the order of reloading progression. The dies need to be properly adjusted for this and the powder dispenser needs to be calibrated to throw the *exact* amount of powder required. Primer seating must be inspected at that particular stage, to verify that the primers are seated to the proper depth.

Sounds great, right, getting all those steps done with one pull of the lever? It is, to an extent. However, a progressive press does not afford the attention to detail that many reloaders both need and enjoy. It is ultimately up to you to decide whether the single-stage process, as outlined above, or the progressive route will work best for you.

For most of my rifle work and some of my pistol work, I prefer the single-stage process. My end results are often more uniform. I do use a progressive press for some pistol calibers, and I like what mine does. It is a great help when you are shooting 300 to 500 pistol rounds in the course of a week, but the progressive press is not perfect. If you do use one, you should weigh the powder charge being dispensed every 10 rounds or so, to be sure it is on the mark. Progressives also often use a primer feed tube to deliver the primers to the correct position and, if a primer isn't fed properly, the risk of primer detonation is real. One primer exploding can set off others, and that is a dangerous proposition. I actually prefer to use a hand primer, as it gives me the surety that all primers are seated to a uniform depth and eliminates the risk of multiple primer detonation. Bullet seating depth, explained in the following chapter, is also an area to be watched, as is the crimp of the case mouth. Uniformity is crucial, especially in a pistol cartridge, where a deviation of 0.1 or 0.2 grains can

result in excessive pressures. Even with all those cautions in hand, the progressives of today, made by Redding, Dillon, RCBS, and others have certainly come a long way. Tolerances are tighter and, therefore, the loaded cartridges are more uniform. Constant inspection, measuring, and checking will help avoid any potential problems.

The application should dictate the type of process that will work for you. Either way, all of the steps outlined above are necessary. Providing that you followed them, you are now ready to being the loading process!

CHAPTER 5

PUTTING YOUR HANDLOAD TOGETHER

Alcohol and gunpowder do not mix!

Let's make some cartridges! If you've followed the steps in Chapter 4, your cleaned brass is resized, de-primed, trimmed, and flared if necessary. It is time to bring your creation to life (insert mad scientist maniacal laughter).

The very first thing you need to do is make sure that only the components you intend to use are on your reloading bench, to avoid any possible mix-ups. Using the wrong type and/or wrong amount of powder, the wrong primer, or the wrong caliber or weight of bullet can create a very dangerous and sometimes deadly combination. The loading of ammunition *requires your undivided attention* and the rules and recipes must be followed strictly. This means no cell phones, no TV, no distracting children, no cigarettes/cigars, and certainly no alcohol or other forms of impairing recreation.

Reading the loading notes for your cartridge in the reloading manual thoroughly will help you to understand which components were used during testing to arrive at the published data. While you may be able to change components once you become a more experienced reloader (and know that changing any of the components in the published recipe requires you to lower the powder charge down to the starting weight, so excessive pressures are not produced), as a new reloader, this is not the time to experiment.

You're going to assemble your cartridges in the same order in which the firing process takes place: primer to powder to bullet.

Priming from the press.

PRIMING THE CASE

Using the appropriate type of primer called for in the reloading manual and count out the number of primers you'll need for the cases you are going to load. Double-check that they are the correct type, as Large Rifle primers are the same size as Large Pistol primers, likewise Small Rifle and Small Pistol. I place my selected primer's in the primer tray, to keep the little buggers from rolling all over the bench. Be sure you a using the correct priming tool size to install the primers, be they Large or Small.

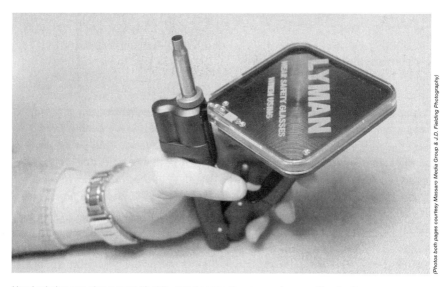
Hand priming can give a good "feel," when it comes to proper primer seating depth.

(Photos both pages courtesy Massaro Media Group & J.D. Fielding Photography)

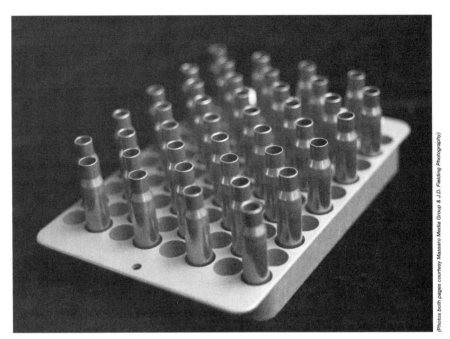

These .308 Winchester cases in the loading block have been primed and are ready for the next step in the reloading process.

(Photos both pages courtesy Massaro Media Group & J.D. Fielding Photography)

If you are using the type of priming tool that attaches to your press, insert the correct shellholder into the ram, place a clean case into it, and extend the ram upward by lowering the handle. Place a new primer into the priming tool, push the priming tool into the slot in the ram that's under the resized case, and lower the case onto the new primer. If you are using a handheld priming tool, slide the case into the shellholder built into the tool, place a new primer in the holder, and give the device a good squeeze.

As much as I use the priming tool on my press, I would honestly recommend that you begin with a handheld primer. You'll be able to "feel" the seating better. Too, while the press gives an enormous mechanical ad-

vantage, it takes quite a bit of time to get the consistent results you're after.

Use just enough force to seat the new primer into the case either perfectly flush or just slightly recessed. Be careful, because a primer that is recessed more than 0.004-inch (see, I said just slightly) could render the primer useless, because the anvil will be crushed. (Your firing pin might also not make contact with a primer seated too deeply, even if that deep seating didn't crush the anvil.) I like primers that are seated flush to the bottom of the rim face, as there are no worries about protrusion or crushed anvils. You *never* want a primer to extend past the face of the rim. This is a dangerous situation, as the possibility of an accidental discharge exists when the bolt face closes on the protruding primer. Checking each primed case for proper seating depth is a necessary step. I run my fingernail over each case after I prime them, then set them on a piece of Melamine that

Keep only one powder at a time on your reloading bench, to avoid any possibility of confusion.

I have screwed down on my reloading bench. Any case that does not sit perfectly on the board or rocks in the slightest bit is inspected to ensure that the primer is properly seated. I prime all the cases I am going to load at one time during that session and place them into the loading block, mouths up, and then move onto the next step in the reloading process.

If, for some reason, a primer is installed incorrectly, you can very, *very* gently use the resizing die to push the primer out of the resized case. You should safely discard the primer that was installed incorrectly, rather than try to reuse it.

CHARGING THE CASE

It is now time to place a new powder charge into the case. You'll need a supply of the powder you intend to use (remember, only one type on the bench at a time), a static-free powder funnel, a powder scale (either beam or digital), and your

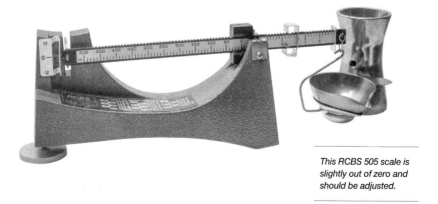

This RCBS 505 scale is slightly out of zero and should be adjusted.

reloading manual to confirm you have the correct powder weight.

Becoming completely familiar with your powder scale is paramount. Read and reread the instruction manual on zeroing and weighing until you are completely confident in how to do this. This is the one reloading tool you don't want to fail on you. The results could be deadly. Have no fear of being overly cautious regarding your scale. While most will give you a lifetime of service without issue, it always pays to check and recheck.

Once your powder scale is set up, be sure to zero the scale. This assures that the powder being measured is the required amount and not a false reading. A set of accurately calibrated scale weights will help boost your confidence in the accuracy of your scale. They are a worthy investment.

Check the zero of the scale every 10 rounds or so when using a beam scale, more often for a digital scale, as some of the inexpensive digital scales tend to drift from zero easily.

If you are using a mechanical powder dispenser, it must be calibrated to drop the correct amount of powder. There is usually a set screw or micrometer that displays the amount of powder being dispensed. This is a *rough* guide, as the different types of powder—spherical, stick, etc.—will dispense differently. With these dispensers, the powder is dumped into the tray on the scale. The powder must then be weighed in order to be sure it is truly an amount consistent with that required. I like to set the dispenser to give a bit less than the desired amount, and then use a powder trickler to dial in the exact amount required.

(Photos both pages courtesy Massaro Media Group & J.D. Fielding Photography)

Scooping powder by hand.

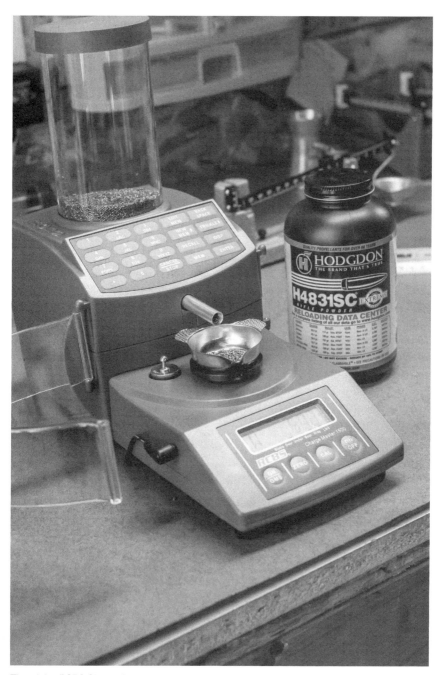

The mighty RCBS ChargeMaster.

In lieu of a dispenser, I scoop powder into the tray by hand. I have several manufactured scoops and homemade varieties to choose from, depending on the cartridge for which I'm loading. For example, the .38 Special uses somewhere around 3.5 grains of powder, the .30-06 Springfield somewhere in the 50- to 55-grain range, while the .416 Rigby and .460 Weatherby use well over 100 grains of powder, so different scoops for different applications. Once I get the charge weight close, I finish it by using the powder trickler for that last tiny bit of powder.

Some folks (including me) enjoy using a digital powder dispenser, such as the RCBS ChargeMaster. It combines an electronic dispenser and digital scale into one unit. It has a large plastic hopper to store the powder you are using and a worm screw-style threaded tube that spins to dispense the powder into the tray. Overall, it looks very similar to the powder trickler device, but it's activated by an electronic motor. You simply enter the charge weight desired on the keypad and the machine dispenses that exact amount. It is easily programmable and capable of storing a number of your favorite loads. It also has a feature I like very much, a repeatable dispensing option that refills the powder tray every time you empty it. It even keeps a count of the number of powder charges dispensed, so you can compare it to the number of cases you've filled. Again, the digital scale on the unit must be frequently zeroed to maintain a consistent powder charge. Even with all the advantages this device offers, I still check the dispensed weight of powder on my balance beam scale every five or 10 rounds to be sure the digital scale hasn't lost zero or drifted at all. As much as the electronic age is convenient, I'm a firm believer in the philosophy of "gravity never wears out," and I trust the simple beam scale above all else! Call me old-fashioned, I guess.

Now, when you have the correct weight of powder on the scale, the powder funnel is placed over the case mouth and the powder is *carefully* poured into the case. Keep a small brush and dust pan in the area in case you have any spills; *never* use

(Photo courtesy Massaro Media Group & J.D. Fielding Photography)

Carefully dispense the powder into the case.

a vacuum for gunpowder or primers, as the static electricity can cause an ignition within the vacuum.

At this time, I'd like to talk about a practice I've developed over the years, one I'm sure I'm going to get some flak from the high-volume pistol reloaders. I charge only one case a time and then move on to seat the bullet. It's a tedious way of doing things, but here's a scenario that may make you adopt this practice.

I've seen (at my local Sheriff's office) a .45 ACP handgun literally blown in two. The cause was a case that was double-charged with powder. The .45 ACP and many other pistol cases have the capacity to hold more than twice the recommended powder and, if you are slightly distracted or simply count which cases you've charged incorrectly, you have a bomb in your hands. The opposite applies to rifles. I've seen a shooter at the range fire his rifle, only to hear a funny "pop" instead of the usual loud report. The shooter ejected the case and saw that the primer was struck and the bullet was gone. My dad, ol' Grumpy Pants, started screaming at the guy to stop, when the gentleman started to load another round. The poor fella looked shocked, had no idea why GP was yelling at him. See, that particular round he'd just fired had *no* powder in it. But the force of the primer had been just enough to lodge that round's bullet into the rifling of the barrel. Had he squeezed off another round, the second bullet would have slammed into the first and, quite possibly, have created pressures large enough to blow up the barrel and, maybe, the shooter. A cleaning rod (and a mallet) safely removed the first bullet, and you can bet the shooter was happy to leave with his only injury being a dent to his pride.

The way I load powder—one case at a time and then seating the bullet—allows me to visually inspect the load before seating the bullet. I have to see an empty case before I use the funnel, then I have to see powder in the case before I seat a bullet.

SEATING THE BULLET

Now that you have the proper amount of powder in your case, let's move onto the last phase.

For this step you will need the bullet seating die and the tools to adjust it, along with your micrometer and enough bullets for the cases you are going to load.

When I'm first starting a loading session, I often make a dummy round, a case without a primer or powder (and plainly marked so), so that, if my seating dies need to be adjusted, I can establish the proper length with a minimum of effort. If I load several different bullets for the same cartridge, I make a dummy round for each bullet, labeling accordingly.

With the ram extended upward, the bullet seating die is screwed down into the press until the rim of the die touches the shellholder. The die is then backed off at least one full turn. The die's lock ring should now be tightened to secure the die's depth. Loosen the seating plug rod located on the top of the die, then raise (un-

The bullet seating process.

The finished product, a newly created, properly dimensioned cartridge!

screw) the rod until the bullet seater is at its highest position.

Gently place a bullet into the case mouth and extend the ram upward. Lower the bullet seater until you feel it make contact with the meplat (nose) of the bullet. Next, lower the ram and screw the bullet seater down two or three turns. Raise the ram again, now seating the bullet further into the case. Lower the ram, remove the cartridge and, using the micrometer, measure the cartridge overall length (COL). Compare the measured length to the COL figure given in the reloading manual for the load you're using. If the cartridge is too long, you must lower the seating die until you achieve the proper length—yes, this is step by step, trial and error process. If the bullet has been seated too deep, I use the bullet puller or inertia

This .38 Special case wasn't properly flared. As a result, the seating process tore the case wall.

(Photos both pages courtesy Massaro Media Group & J.D. Fielding Photography)

hammer to remove the bullet from the case and start the procedure again until I have achieved a cartridge of the proper COL dimension.

Once the die has been properly set up to give the desired seating depth, you can start the process of seating bullets into the cases that have the powder charge in place. Measure each cartridge for length with the micrometer and place the loaded cartridges into your storage box.

For the pistol calibers, it is extremely important that you strictly adhere to the COL published values, especially when they're being used in an autoloading pistol. This dimension will allow the cartridges to feed properly and keep pressures in line with the manual. In a revolver, following the published data will give you cartridges that fit the cylinder perfectly,

with no over-length issues that will either prevent you from properly closing the cylinder or have the revolver lock up thanks to a pulled bullet. (A "pulled" bullet, also known as a bullet that's "pulled crimp" is one that unseats and moves forward slightly out of the case during the recoil generated from another cartridge being fired. It's a phenomenon that mostly happens with large-bore revolvers, and, when it does, the bullet can extend past the cylinder face, preventing the cylinder from turning and even from being opened up without some serious force applied. In all, you *really* don't want this to happen.)

For rifle shooters, bullet seating depth can have a great affect on the performance of the rifle. A wealth of information has been exchanged about the benefits of seating the bul-

Mono-metal bullets are usually longer than their copper and lead counterparts, as they are constructed of a lighter metal than lead.

(Photos both pages courtesy Massaro Media Group & J.D. Fielding Photography)

let in the case at a depth of 0.015-inch or less off the lands and grooves of the rifling, in order to attain superior accuracy. The idea is to minimize the amount of "jump" the bullet has from the case mouth to the rifled portion of the barrel. This is a very complicated technique and, if done improperly, can result in a pressure spike that can be detrimental to your health and your rifle. You *never* want the bullet to be touching the rifle barrel's lands before it's been fired. Too, seating the bullets too far out will often prevent your cartridges from fitting into the magazine of your rifle. Forward-seating rifle bullets is a technique best left to the most experienced loaders. Heck, I fall into the "most experienced" category and I avoid the practice altogether. I firmly believe that the best level

of safety and accuracy can be found with a proper COL and the habit of weighing out your projectiles into uniform groups, and I like to adhere to overall lengths that do not exceed the SAAMI specifications.

Note that, in addition to the general rule of keeping your COL to that recommended in your reloading manual, some of the all-copper or gilding metal rifle bullets such as the Barnes TSX, Hornady GMX, or Nosler E-Tip can be *very* sensitive to seating depth. With these premium bullets, a slight variation of the seating depth of the bullet can have a *drastic* effect on accuracy. Yes, some experimentation with different seating depths is often called for and, when the magic depth is found, these can be among the most accurate bullets available—but sometimes an

106 Gun Digest Shooter's Guide to Reloading

adjustment of 0.1-inch will make or break your group. I suggest you contact the bullet manufacturer for their recommended seating depths and safe practices with these mono-metal bullets, if the SAAMI maximum length does not give you the accuracy you desire; when you do find the proper seating depth with these particular bullets in your rifle, be sure and keep accurate records, so you can reproduce the recipe!

Seating your bullets too *deep* in a rifle cartridge case is a problem for any rifle bullet. Doing so will cause pressures to rise, so, again, be sure to use the micrometer to maintain a COL consistent with the test data in your reloading manual.

If a bullet has a "cannelure," that ring around it near the base that's often grooved, I believe it is best to seat the bullet so that the case mouth is halfway up the cannelure from the base of the bullet. This depth of seating is most often the one the bullet company used when it performed its testing; if you're using a reloading book produced by your bullet's maker, you should find that the data in the reloading manual will closely match your own findings.

CRIMPING

Some cartridges require that their bullets be crimped into the case mouth, to ensure the forces of recoil or rapid loading don't force the bullet to move. The rimmed and/or straight-walled cases that are so popular in the lever-action rifles are one example, and many of the common revolver rounds are another.

These .45 Colt cartridges were roll crimped, so the bullets won't move out of the case under recoil, when fired in a revolver.

A heavy roll crimp was placed on the case mouths of this .458 Winchester Magnum (left) and the noticeably bigger .500 Nitro Express.

(Photo courtesy Massaro Media Group & J.D. Fielding Photography)

Most of our favorite lever-action rifles feature a tubular magazine, and the bullets, while lined up nose to tail in the magazine, can be driven into the case mouth from the recoil generated from firing. In the case of the revolver, as I've already noted, the opposite holds true: the bullets can move out past the case mouth from the recoil.

To combat the movement of the bullets, the very edge of the case mouth is rolled into the bullet's cannelure. This is known, aptly enough, as "roll crimping." The hard-recoiling "safari" cartridges are often crimped, to be sure that the bullets don't move in the case when in the magazine of a bolt-action rifle or in the second barrel of a double rifle. Many early reports of the .458 Winchester Magnum claimed that the heavy recoil of this cartridge would often drive the bullets down into the cartridge case, resulting in heavily compressed loads, which produced much lower than normal velocities. I've never personally experienced this, but I also have no reason to doubt the stories. Oh, and one thing more than worth noting about this subject: I want to state here that any bullet that does *not* have a cannelure should *never* be crimped, as you can damage the case and bullet trying to do so.

In order to use your seating die to seat the bullet and place a roll crimp on the case, follow this procedure:

With a cleaned and resized (and flared, if necessary) case, seat the bullet as described in the section above, so that the COL is as desired.

Then, back the seating plug (turn it counterclockwise) out of the die to its highest setting. Next, with cartridge and ram extended fully upward, loosen the lock ring and the seating die, then screw the seating die down until you feel the top of the die barely "bite" on the case mouth. Lower the ram and screw the die down an eighth of turn. When you extend the ram upward again, you should see the roll crimp on the bullet cannelure. It may take several tries (and several cases) until you get it right. Don't get upset, you'll iron it out. Once the roll crimp is adjusted properly, raise the ram again and lower the seating plug until you just feel it touching the top of the bullet. Now, back the ram off and lower the seating plug an eighth to a quarter of a turn. The next cartridge you make should both seat and crimp in the same stroke. Use the micrometer to verify the COL.

Be careful and read your reloading manual, as not all cartridges can be roll crimped. The uber-popular .45 ACP, for example, headspaces off the case mouth and must use a *taper* crimp to ensure proper loading and firing. The taper crimp doesn't roll the brass over into a cannelure, rather it squeezes the mouth portion of the case tightly against the bullet. This technique firmly holds the bullet in place, yet maintains the square-cut case mouth that allows the case to be properly headspaced in the firearm's chamber. Several companies make a taper crimping die, separate from all the others previously described.

For all your loading sessions, be sure and record your work. It will be a great reference for the future and help you keep track of how your loads performed when you take them to the range. For example:

17 October 2013

.30-06 Springfield, Winchester Model 70 Featherweight

Remington cases, third loading, 20 cases

CCI 200 Large Rifle primer

Nosler 165-grain Ballistic Tip

55.0 grains IMR4350

COL = 3.340 inches

Range results: 100-yard three-shot group spread of 0.85-inch, 2,725 fps on chronograph, no pressure signs.

22 October 2013

.30-06 Springfield, Winchester Model 70 Featherweight

Federal cases, first loading, 20 cases

Federal 210 Large Rifle primer

Hornady 220-grain InterLock

52.5 grains of Reloder-19

COL = 3.340 inches

Range results: 100-yard three-shot group average spread of 2.5 inches, 2,420 fps on chronograph, slight pressure signs.

Not very inspiring, can do better.

Entries such as these will help you replicate the best results and eliminate the clunkers. It will also give you an idea of how many firings you're getting from your brass, what loads your guns like best, whether or not your loads are approaching dangerous pressure, and so on and so forth. My notebook is invaluable to me.

CHAPTER 6

WHAT TO BUY

In Chapter 5, I covered the basic process of loading a cartridge. Now I wish to discuss the numerous types of components currently available to the loader, help explain their differences, and discuss some ways to use them effectively. The reloading process itself has remained relatively unchanged since the days of O'Connor and Keith, but some of the components we have available to us today would have gained their attention in a heartbeat!

What follows is a cross-section of some of the advancements and changes in reloading products. Hopefully it will help you decide on a place to start as a new handloader, then provide a pathway for experimentation, as you learn and become more confident both in your loads and how they perform in your firearms.

PRIMERS

For the most part, the primers of 30 years ago are relatively unchanged today. This is a good thing. Being able to count upon consistent ignition, without corrosion, is often taken for granted. Whichever of the major manufacturers' products you choose, I believe you can count upon a repeatable scenario. CCI, Federal, Remington, and Winchester all make very reliable products, for a wide range of applications. Some smaller and lesser known companies also have primers available as components. TulAmmo and MagTech both

Federal Gold Medal Large Rifle primers.
(Photo courtesy Massaro Media Group & J.D. Fielding Photography)

A wide variety of .375-inch caliber bullets.

make a full line of rifle and pistol primers, while Fiocchi (best known for its shotgun ammunition), also offers Small Rifle and Small Pistol primers.

The bottom line to primers is this. Primers are the ignition system of any cartridge and, without a healthy supply, you're out of business. They can't be reused or refurbished. Once you settle on a brand and type that works for you, I advise you pick up at least a couple thousand to be sure you have a good supply on hand. Keep them in a cool, dry place and they'll stay good almost indefinitely.

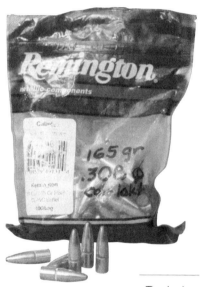

The classic Remington Core-Lokt.

RIFLE BULLETS

Unlike primers, bullet technology has progressed leaps and bounds in the last three decades. There's a lot to cover here. Let's look at rifle bullets first.

Some gun writers, like Jack O'Connor, trusted in the rapid expansion of light-for-caliber bullets to dispatch game. Elmer Keith liked the deep penetration of heavy-for-caliber bullets to take large animals. Both camps have their followers, kind of a Chevy versus Ford thing. I subscribe to both, in varying degrees and depending on the job at hand.

An early box of Winchester Silvertips, in .348 Winchester.

Speer bullets have always been a good value.

The classic bullets that started it all are still with us, very much alive and well and still well-loved and much used to this day. These include Hornady's Interlock, Sierra's GameKings, Pro-Hunters, and MatchKings, Winchester's Power-Point, Remington's Core-Lokt, and Speer's Hot-Cor, to name a few. I can remember ol' Grumpy Pants waxing poetically about the premium rifle bullets of his youth: The Winchester SilverTip, the Nosler Partition, and the Speer Grand Slam.

They were and are great bullets and, with the exception of the SilverTip, they are still with us. (The Winchester SilverTip was a traditional cup-and-core bullet, with the nose covered by a harder metal to ensure deep penetration.) The Grand Slam from Speer uses a lead core of varying hardness, so as to better hold together for deep penetration. This bullet is still available, and it performs very well. Speer's Hot-Cor bullet is also still available, and Speer has introduced a new bonded-core Deep Curl bullet, for higher weight retention. Speer's TNT line of varmint bullets possess the frangible qualities a good varmint bullet should.

The late John Nosler was very unhappy with the shallow penetration of traditional cup-and-core bullets run out of his .300 Holland & Hol-

The Nosler Partition, the premium bullet that started it all.

land and impacted on the shoulder of a large moose. Necessity being the mother of invention, he drilled out a copper rod from both ends, crimped the nose section, and filled the jacket with lead, leaving a copper "partition" in the center. The front half of the bullet would

An array of Barnes bullets, including the TSX and TTSX.

(Photos both pages courtesy Massaro Media Group & J.D. Fielding Photography)

expand in a familiar manner, while the shank portion of the bullet behind the partition would continue to penetrate deep into the game animal. This performance was unprecedented. Today, the Nosler Partition continues as a staple in the hunting world, and it's one I use to this day.

In more recent history, there have been some innovative and downright wonderful new bullet designs. Perhaps the most radical has been the

Barnes X, now updated to the Triple Shock (TSX). Fred Barnes founded the company, priding himself in creating heavy-for-caliber bullets that would penetrate. The company went through hard times and was eventually purchased by Randy and Coni Brooks, in the 1980s. Randy Brooks had a revolutionary idea whilst hunting brown bears: Remove the soft lead from the equation and use only the harder copper gilding metal. That design was offered in a hollowpoint configuration, which would expand upon contact and create what resembled the letter "X" after expansion. Overall, the bullet offered a combination of rapid expansion and deep penetration.

I must go on the record as saying that the initial design of this bullet intrigued me, but I couldn't get it to shoot well. It also left an extraordinary amount of copper fouling in my rifle's bore; being all copper and, thus, lighter than lead, the bullet was longer than its cup-and-core counterparts and, so, had more bearing surface on the rifling. I tried several different calibers and bullet weights of the Barnes X, but to no avail. I just could not get the accuracy level out of them I demand from my rifles and, because of this, I abandoned them for a good while.

Things might have changed for me and the Barnes bullet. Several of my customers have recently ordered some of the revised Triple Shock (TSX) projectiles, which, in effect, forced me to take another look at the idea. As explained in a recent conversation with the good Mr. Brooks,

Expanded and recovered .416-caliber 400-grain bullets, used to take a Cape buffalo, in Zambia.

(Photo courtesy Massaro Media Group & J.D. Fielding Photography)

he revamped the design by cutting grooves in the bullet's shank of the bullet, thereby reducing fouling. It not only did that quite well, accuracy was greatly improved! Overall, the TSX from Barnes is an accurate, deep-penetrating, and dependable big-game bullet. It has a great reputation across the globe. We now also have the Barnes TTSX (Tipped Triple Shock X), a similar all-copper bullet, but with a pointed polymer tip. Both designs will deliver the dependable penetration we hunters all desire, easily reaching the vitals, and, when properly loaded, they will deliver pinpoint accuracy. I think the only bone of contention I have with them is that the seating depth has a great deal of influence on their accuracy, but, once the proper depth is found, you'll have a lifetime of good accuracy and killing power. I really enjoy these bullets

when loading the lighter-for-caliber recipes, as they will attain the high velocity of a light bullet, yet still hold together and penetrate like a much heavier bullet. The 130-grain .308-inch diameter, 160-grain .338-inch diameter, and 235-grain .375-inch diameter are among my favorites.

Building upon the idea of a partitioned bullet, Swift's Bill Hober decided to improve their performance by chemically bonding the copper jacket to the hard lead core. Presto! The Swift A-Frame was born. The front portion expands to two times the caliber, and the portion behind the partition almost always rivets during penetration. Weight retention is often over 90 percent. I have taken dozens of species of game on the North American and African continents with this bullet, and I believe it to be one of the best available to the

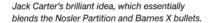

Jack Carter's brilliant idea, which essentially blends the Nosler Partition and Barnes X bullets.

A polymer-tipped version of the Trophy Bonded Bear Claw.

big-game hunter. This bullet can produce sub-MOA groups, even in the big safari calibers. I can best describe this bullet as "meat resistant," that is, the more meat it hits, the more it opens and disperses its energy.

I've used a 300-grain, .375-inch diameter Swift A-Frame bullet on an 1,800-pound bison on the Great Plains, recovering the bullet at 92-percent weight retention. This same bullet *whistles* through a diminutive African steenbok, producing little expansion or meat damage, yet still killing quickly and cleanly. In my humble opinion, the 400-grain .416-caliber Swift A-Frame, delivered from either a .416 Remington or .416 Rigby, makes the ideal Cape buffalo medicine. The A-Frame really shines on the bigger and nastier creatures and, if you're looking to beef up the performance of your favorite deer

rifle for use on larger game, this is an excellent choice.

Jack Carter also modified the partition idea, this time by removing all the lead behind the partition to leave nothing but solid copper in the rear of the bullet. The Trophy Bonded Bear Claw is what's known as a "bonded bullet," with lead in the nose area only and solid copper billet in the rear. It hits hard and holds together very well. The Bear Claw is an accurate bullet. It is currently loaded by the Federal Cartridge Company and available as a component. There is also a polymer-tipped variety, engineered to give a better B.C.

For many years, big-game hunters envied the benchrest crowd's accuracy with their "match-grade" bullets. These bullets were often hollowpoint boat-tails, constructed with nothing more (and nothing less!)

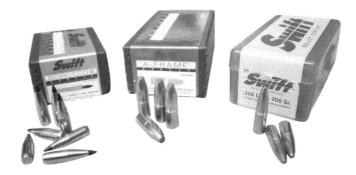

Nosler has a wide selection of premium bullets, enough to satisfy the whole gamut of shooters' needs.

than precision in mind. Penetration and expansion mattered not, because paper was the intended target. Some hunters tried using uber-accurate match bullets on game, with poor result; the bullets lacked the strength for suitable penetration. Enter the good folks from Nosler again. They used the hollowpoint boat-tail design, but this time with a thicker, jacket and a sharp polymer tip in the hollow cavity intended to initiate proper expansion. Today, hunters have been enjoying the Ballistic Tip for more than two decades. It is best used on game from the size of pronghorn antelope to caribou; bullets for bigger, tougher game are best left to the Partition realm. Ballistic Tips are exceptionally accurate.

North Fork bonded-core semi-spitzers and cup solids.

There is also another similar Nosler offering called the Accubond. It looks quite like a Ballistic Tip, but, instead of a nose tip color-coded by caliber, the Accubond is bedecked in white and the core is chemically bonded to the jacket to prevent separation. From the small- and medium-game calibers to the mighty .375-inch bore, the Accubond is capable of good accuracy and trajectory, while still holding together. Nosler also has its Custom Competition series, specifically created with the target shooter in mind. These are comprised of precision drawn jackets and a long boat-tail for the high B.C. paper-punchers love so much. They are a match-grade hollowpoint, designed for use on paper only, and are not recommended for hunting applications. They are a serious contender when uber-accuracy is desired.

Bill Hober at Swift wasn't done, when he created the A-Frame. His Scirocco II could be described as a Ballistic Tip on steroids. Designed as a hunting bullet with a much thicker jacket than other bullets and, like the Nosler Accubond, with a chemically bonded core, this long lean beast is also exceptionally accurate. Weight retention is not that far behind the A-Frame, and the very high ballistic coefficient makes the trajectory flat. I've seen some hunting rifles give benchrest accuracy with these bullets, and they hit hard. I used a 180-grain Scirocco II out of my .308 Winchester to crumple a 200-plus-pound Canadian black bear like he'd been a piece of typing paper.

Originally out of Wyoming, the North Fork Bullet Company of Or-

The Scirocco II is capable of producing very fine accuracy.

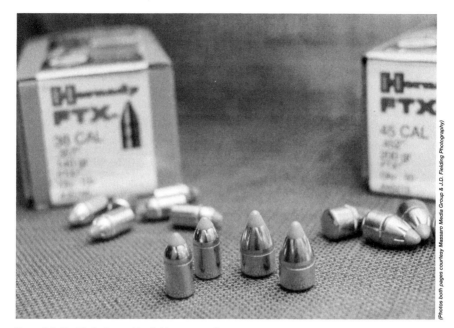

Hornady's FlexTip bullets, with pliable nose section.

egon has some rather unique designs in its lineup. The flagship of the fleet is the Bonded Core Soft Point, a semi-spitzer that balances its weight toward the front of the bullet. The shank of the bullet has a series of minute grooves, designed to reduce fouling and keep pressures low. These bullets are constructed of pure copper and pure lead, for deep penetration and weight retention. They are a *great* hunting bullet choice. For those headed across the pond for the big nasties, North Fork offers a Flat Point Solid and a Cup Point Solid. Both are mono-metal bullets, but the Cup Point has an indentation in the nose section, creating an "expanding solid," if you will. The goal is to have a slight deformation in the frontal section for larger-than-caliber expansion, while retaining the classic, straight-line penetration of a solid bullet. I like this idea for a follow-up shot on Cape buffalo, because everyone knows how cranky those guys are when they've got a bullet in them and haven't decided to die yet. North Fork also offers a Percussion Point, a bullet scored at the nose to initiate more rapid expansion on the great cats, thus imparting hydrostatic shock to dispatch lions, and leopards, notorious for being undead when you least need them to be. They would also make a great deer bullet, in my opinion.

The folks at Hornady have been busy lately. I think its FlexTip line is a really neat idea. Ammunition for lever-action rifles and their tubular magazines has been limited to flat-tipped or round-nosed bullets, to eliminate the possibility of having

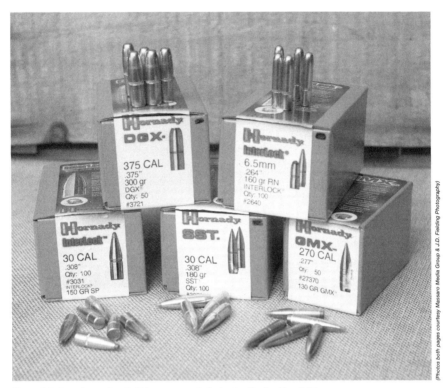

Hornady's line of premium bullets are a great choice for the hunting fields.

the pointed nose of a sharp spitzer bullet punch the primer of the bullet in front of it in the tube and causing a chain-fire magazine detonation. The problem with round- and flat-nosed bullets is that they lose their velocity and, therefore, their energy, rather quickly downrange. That's why most lever-actions are considered to have limited effective range. That all changed when Hornady developed a pliable, rubbery nose and put it on a spitzer bullet, thereby solving both the problems of magazine chain-fire and limited range. There is no risk of magazine detonation, and the classics now benefit from the better trajectory and striking energy of the spitzer bullet. Grandpa's old .30-30 WCF gets

a whole new take on life, and I'm even seeing these classic lever guns on the Great Plains used for hunting pronghorn!

Hornady also has revamped its bigger caliber bullets, introducing what it calls the DGX and DGS bullets (Dangerous Game eXpanding and Dangerous Game Solid). They are loaded in Hornady's factory ammunition and are also available as component parts for the African hunter or those looking to pursue the great bears.

While famous for its cup-and-core InterLock bullet, which is an old, proven faithful, Hornady has now added the SST, essentially the Interlock with a red polymer tip that prevents any

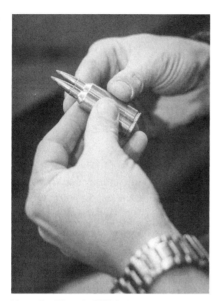

Hornady 150-grain GMX bullets loaded in the .270 Winchester Short Magnum.

All three are all approved for use in those areas that ban the use of lead bullets. Both the GMX and E-Tip are polymer-tipped spitzers, and accurate ones at that. Like the TSX, the GMX and E-Tip are longer in any given caliber/weight than a cup-and-core of the same weight, but, loaded properly, they are very effective bullets.

The folks at Sierra have been making wonderfully accurate bullets since the late 1940s. The Sierra MatchKing series is, in a simple turn of phrase, the benchmark of rifle accuracy. They have been available for decades, originally offered as a FMJ configuration and now revised to the very well-known boat-tail or flat-base hollowpoint design that has set so many target records and been responsible for some incredible long-range shots. The .30-caliber 168-grain MatchKing is, perhaps, the most inherently accurate of the bunch. My bud Mark "Pig Newton"

damage to the lead nose and improves the downrange ballistics. I've found this bullet to be very accurate and just hell on deer-sized game!

There is a movement to ban the use of lead-core ammunition, spurred on by a large, long state on the West Coast. Without getting political, the unfortunate reality is that there may very well be a lead ban in many other places in the near future. Some answers to this, and certainly options for those target shooters and hunters doing what they do where lead ammo restrictions are already in place, the Barnes TSX is pure copper, as is the Hornady GMX (Gilding Metal eXpanding), and the Nosler E-Tip.

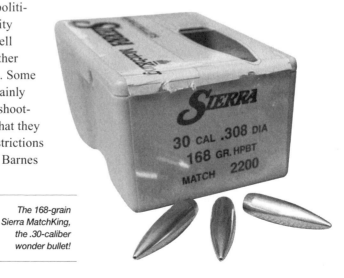

The 168-grain Sierra MatchKing, the .30-caliber wonder bullet!

Nazi has a .308 Winchester that puts these into ¼-MOA, and my .22-250 Remington absolutely loves launching the .224-inch 53-grain flat-base hollowpoint MatchKing through her barrel. When I am developing a load for a rifle I feel might have a questionable barrel, I reach for a Sierra MatchKing in that caliber and start the testing there—they're that good. While they are not recommended for hunting applications, I can tell you that the 53-grain MKs are devastating on coyotes and foxes, when properly placed from my .22-250.

Sierra's hunting bullet lineup has become an old standby. It's kind of funny. I was chatting with my pal Carroll Pillant, from Sierra, at a trade show and asked him what new products were coming out this year. Completely deadpan, he looked at me and said "Nuthin'." When I laughed he said "We can't keep up with customer demand for the bullets we already offer. There's no time to develop a new one." Another way of looking at it is that Sierra bullets work so well there really isn't much need to develop anything new. The Pro-Hunter series of flat-base (both round-nosed and spitzer) bullets are a solid choice for hunting, and the GameKing spitzer boat-tails have a well-earned reputation for long-range accuracy and hitting hard. There is a polymer-tipped BlitzKing available for the lighter calibers and designed for rapid expansion, along with many hollowpoint designs to round out a full line of varmint bullets.

One of my favorite bullets from Sierra is Part No. 2140, the .308-inch 165-grain HPBT GameKing. It's

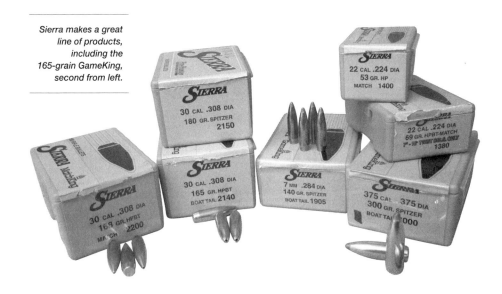

Sierra makes a great line of products, including the 165-grain GameKing, second from left.

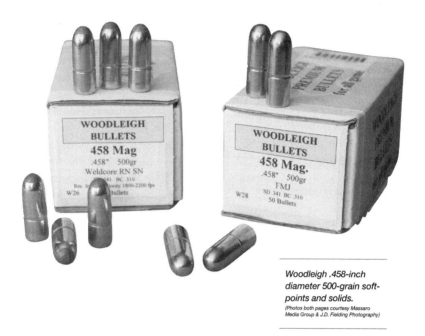

Woodleigh .458-inch diameter 500-grain soft-points and solids.
(Photos both pages courtesy Massaro Media Group & J.D. Fielding Photography)

designed after the 168-grain Match-King, but with an appropriately thick jacket for hunting. The hollowpoint nose is crimped shut, sort of in the form of an "X." Bottom line, this is a *devastating* deer bullet. Kevin Hicks uses it in his WWII-era 03-A3 Springfield named "Autumn," and I've used it extensively in my .308 Winchester. Both rifles print well under a single MOA with it and have accounted for numerous deer in Upstate New York. It has great accuracy, with good penetration and expansion. Good job, Sierra!

Woodleigh Bullets from Australia isn't a new company, and while you may not have heard of them, they hold a very important place among the bullet maker crowd. For those of us with vintage rifles, especially double rifles of European design and which were regulated with the British Kynoch ammo, we turn to Woodleigh for bullets that are of proper dimension. You see, Kynoch was out of commission for a few decades, and Woodleigh filled the niche. It allowed the collectors and shooters of those classic guns to drag them out of mothballs and get them out to the range and game fields again. The Woodleigh Weldcore is a round-nosed bonded-core bullet that has gained a respectable reputation going up against heavy, thick-skinned animals. I have also read about a "hydrostatically stabilized" solid that has a cupped front and a banded shank, designed for a large wound channel and straight-line penetration. To the African hunter, the bullet choices have never been better!

Berger Bullets are one of the newly popular companies offering both match-grade target bullets and

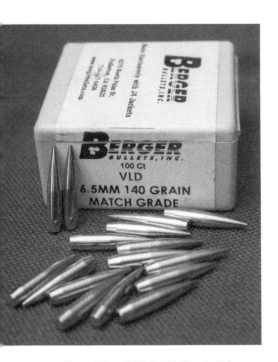

Berger 6.5mm (.264-inch) 140-grain VLD
bullets. Long and lean, these bullets have a
very high B.C. and are wonderfully accurate.

extremely accurate hunting bullets.
From The VLD (Very Low Drag) line
of hunting bullets to the very heavy-
for-caliber boat-tail match offerings,
Berger Bullets and its J4 match-grade
jackets can and will produce impressive results. I have had very good results with Berger bullets in my friend
Le Frogg's .17 Remington, especially
with the heavier 30-grain model. It
easily creates the deadly "red mist"
on woodchucks out to 350 yards.
These bullets are very consistent and
well known for their accuracy.

Precision Ballistics is a maker of
hand-swaged and -assembled premium
bullets for the competition shooter. They
are available in 6mm and 6.5mm only,
but produce some extremely impressive

results in rifles of this bore size. They
feature the Berger J4 jacket (renowned
for its accuracy), and bullet weight is
held to extremely tight tolerances.

John Lazzeroni, famous for the
proprietary magnum rifles that bear his
name, has produced his own projectile
designed to work well in the cartridges
he designed. The LazerHead bullet is
an all-copper hollowpoint boat-tail,
very similar in construction to the
Barnes TSX. I haven't used them yet,
but, after speaking with John and hearing his tales of some very, very long-
range success stories, I look forward to
using them.

Norma has some cool bullets available. The Oryx is a semi-spitzer with
a pure lead core bonded to the jacket.
The jacket is thinner towards the front
of the bullet, getting thicker toward
the rear to retard expansion and retain
weight. Many of my friends who hunt
in Africa swear by this bullet. The
Norma Kalahari is a lead-free hollowpoint bullet of revolutionary shape.
The front portion is designed to break
into six frangible petals to create a
large wound channel, while the rear
portion is designed to penetrate deeply.
The Norma Alaskan is a round-nose
soft-point that performs well and
penetrates deeply. It makes a great
choice on larger game at close ranges.
Norma's Vulkan is a pointed bullet
with a squared meplat, and the jacket
is folded over and crimped into the
core at the nose. The flattened point
gives rapid expansion, while resisting
deformation. Finally, for the largest of
African game, Norma offers its own
Solid bullet. It has a very good reputation among African Professional Hunt-

Left to right, the Norma Oryx, Norma round-nosed Alaskan, and the flat meplat Norma Vulcan.

Left to right, the Lapua Scenar, Lapua's Mega, and Lapua's Naturalis.

ers and would make a good choice for the travelling hunter. They are offered in calibers between 9.3mm (.366-inch) and the behemoth .500 Jeffery and .505 Gibbs.

Lapua offers bullets that are on par with the quality of its legendary brass cases. The Scenar and Scenar-L are among the best target bullets available, both offering extremely tight tolerances and boat-tail hollowpoint construction that benchrest shooters love so much. They are a very accurate target bullet and well respected in the benchrest community.

The Secnars aren't the only bullets Lapua makes. The Mega and the Naturalis are both hunting bullets that are often used in Scandinavia. The Mega is a long, lean, cup-and-core blunt-nosed hunting bullet, offered in 6.5mm, .308, and 9.3mm bore diameters and designed for high weight retention. The Naturalis is comprised of 99-perecent copper, with a hollowpoint capped with a green plastic tip. It's a bit more rounded than the Nosler Ballistic Tip or Swift Scirocco II, but still initiates expansion on the same basic principle.

There is a, well, rather radical bullet company from Pennsylvania named Cutting Edge Bullets, and it isn't afraid to step out of the box. It offers some long-range bullets in the typical configuration of a boat-tail hollowpoint, but these feature a "Sealtite" band. This single band rides on the rifling and forms a positive gas seal, which aids in utilizing all the burning powder in the barrel. There are different configurations, where the Sealtite band is located in different positions depending on its use in a magazine bolt-action guns or for single-shot rifles where the bullet can be seated further out of the case. Very interesting concepts!

Cutting Edge's Safari series is constructed of brass. The Safari Solid is a parallel-sided, solid, flat meplat bullet made for straight-line penetration without expansion. It should prove to work well where a solid is warranted. The Safari Raptor is a brass hollowpoint bullet with six petals that open upon impact. There is an optional polymer plug that can be inserted into the hollow cavity to further initiate expansion and improve the ballistic coefficient of the bullet.

These are but a few of the newer offerings. I couldn't possibly cover them all, and I intend no slight to anyone's product I haven't mentioned, but the point remains: As hunters and shooters who load our own ammunition for our rifles, we can tailor our choice of bullet to the job at hand, and that is the most fun part of handloading for our rifles!

PISTOL AND REVOLVER BULLETS

Pistol bullets have also made great progress. One of the areas with the largest degree of advancement is in the realm of those intended for self-defense.

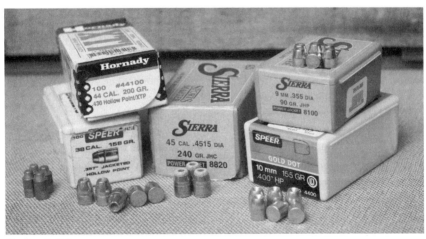

Handgun bullets.

There are many bullets designed for self-defense, such as the Hornady XTP (eXtreme Terminal Performance), the Speer Gold Dot, and the Federal Hydra Shok. The Gold Dot is really nothing more than a very well-constructed jacketed bullet, and it's available in most common handgun calibers. Hornady's XTP and XTP Mag feature a very heavy jacket that helps to control expansion, as well as help the projectiles stand up to higher velocity. My .45 Colt shoots the 300 XTP very well. They are strong enough to be used for backup while hiking or for use during a bear hunt. Finally, the Federal Hydra Shok handgun bullet features a center post, and the jacket is notched to promote expansion for a high energy exchange upon striking the target. Any and all of these are good choices for defense rounds.

For the competition pistol shooter, Hornady's HAP (Hornady Action Pistol) has many of the proven features of the XTP, but it lacks the cannelure and folded copper jacket needed for controlled expansion. Otherwise it has the same dimensions, but it's designed for the very smooth feeding that target shooters require.

Many shooting clubs with indoor ranges don't allow the use of bullets with exposed lead, in order that lead vapors can't become an issue. Rainier Bullets (www.rainierballistics.com), from Washington State, makes pistol bullets that are entirely covered with a copper jacket. According to its

Expanded Speer GoldDot handgun bullet.

An expanded HydroShok, with its center post clearly visible.

The author's sweetheart Ruger Blackhawk .45 Colt with ammunition loaded with 300-grain Hornady XTP bullets.

literature, this can reduce lead vapors by up to 95 percent.

Cutting Edge Bullets has neat pistol bullets, too. The HG Solid, PHD (Personal Home Defense) and Handgun Raptor bullets are comprised of all copper. Both have three or four driving bands on the bullet shank, and while the HG Solid is a solid-copper bullet, the PHD (Personal Home Defense) bullet is a hollowpoint with a deep cavity and is actually designed to be very frangible. Four copper petals open rapidly upon impact and eventually separate from the rear portion of the bullet, for maximum hydrostatic shock. After that petal separation, the rear portion of the bullet continues to drive through, for a devastating wound on the front end of impact, followed by a deep, caliber-sized wound channel.

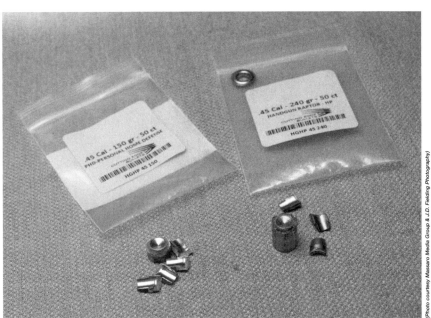

This is Cutting Edge's pistol bullet after impact. The "petals" break away for an initial wound area, then the base travels further for deep penetration.

In this day of ammunition and component scarcity (compounded by the rising cost of copper-clad pistol bullets), the pistol shooter who enjoys putting a large amount of lead downrange each weekend can find themselves in a quandary. Hard-cast lead pistol bullets can provide an available and less expensive answer for the weekend *pistolero*. Falcon Bullet Company, from Tennessee, makes great hard-cast lead bullets, which are affordable and shoot very well. I have used them with great results, in both my .38 Special and .45 Colt revolvers. I have also loaded them in my .45 ACP ammunition and printed very good groups. They are available in a wide variety of calibers and profiles.

It is also possible to cast your own lead pistol bullets, to keep costs down. Lyman and Lee, among others, make good and affordable pistol (and rifle) bullet molds that are fun and simple to use. A good supply of lead,

An The Swift A-Frame pistol bullets, shown in section and expanded.

The Barnes XPB, shown in section and expanded.

some wheel weights for hardness, and a place in the fresh open air to melt the lead can yield a healthy supply of pistol bullets for the range. (I mention to do this in the open air for a reason. You should *never* cast lead bullets indoors. Inhaling the fumes will have you drooling in your oatmeal before you know it. Follow the guidelines for the proper mixture of lead and antimony, melt and mould outdoors, and you should have a bunch of fun shooting your home-made creations!)

For those hunters who prefer to pursue game with a handgun, there are lots of great new hunting bullets available, many constructed in the same manner as rifle bullets.

The Barnes XPB is a pistol variety of the all-copper bullet Barnes is so famous for. Nosler offers the Sporting Handgun Revolver and Sport-ing Handgun Pistol bullets, both well constructed. Swift offers the famous A-Frame in many popular hunting handgun calibers, providing the reliable penetration and expansion needed for those who bring their favorite handgun to the hunting fields. Hornady makes the FTX bullet in many popular revolver calibers, for use in both pistols and rifles that are chambered for those handgun cartridges. The Flex-Tip gives a better ballistic coefficient than round- or flat-nosed bullets, yet is perfectly safe to use in a tubular magazine. Use them in your handgun and they will give you a bit flatter trajectory.

POWDER

Powders, along with bullets, have made some huge technological leaps, but it's worth examining those that

Modern powder comes in an amazing variety.

Left to right: Hodgdon's H4831SC grains are cut shorter to flow better in the powder measurer; Alliant BlueDot is very useful in handgun loads; IMR7828 is a fine choice for magnum cases, as its slow burn rate helps develop high velocities. (Photos both pages courtesy Massaro Media Group & J.D. Fielding Photography)

came before them, because it's not like the powders of yesteryear were bad or inferior. Heck, I use many powders that have been with us since before my dad was born; the IMR series of powders is a classic that instantly comes to mind. The IMR3031, IMR4064, IMR4320 and IMR4350 of my father's youth are still here, still as good as they ever were, and I use them for my own loads and my clients on a daily basis.

Hodgdon's many fantastic powders are still around, although in some improved variations. Its H380, a spherical military surplus powder named for Bruce Hodgdon's famous .22-250 load of 38.0 grains of powder topped with a 55-grain bullet, is alive

and well. It is *the* powder of choice for .22-250, in this author's humble opinion, yet is versatile enough to produce very accurate loads in .308 Winchester and even the new kid on the safari block, the .375 Ruger. H4831 is now offered as H4831SC, the SC standing for "short cut," a shorter-length stick powder designed to better flow through a powder measure. Burn rate and load data remain the same as the older version, yet it is easier to work with.

Winchester's venerable powders like W760 are still thriving, due to the fact that Hodgdon is in charge of not only its own powder line, but also now produces the IMR and Winchester lines.

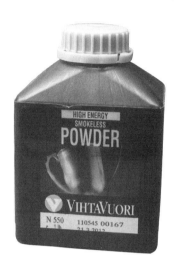

Left to right: IMR8208XBR is very uniform across a wide range of temperatures; Alliant's Power Pro 4000-MR is a good choice for larger capacity cases; Made in Finland, VihtaVuori's N550 is a great option for fueling the venerable .30-06 Springfield and its ilk. (Photo courtesy Massaro Media Group & J.D. Fielding Photography)

The old Hercules Company was bought up by Alliant, and *man*, this company is making great stuff! The classic Reloder series still thrives, as does the pistol/shotgun powders like BlueDot, GreenDot, Unique, and Bullseye.

Old and faithful standbys aside, some of the newer powders have brought both old and new cartridges to the forefront, by giving them the power to show off their case capacity and/or giving them a velocity boost that was previously unobtainable. IMR7828, introduced to reloaders in 1985, can gather very high velocities out of magnum cases, something that couldn't be done with the old IMR powders. This new one is a very slow burning powder and functions best in the big magnum cases and guns with longer barrels.

IMR has also released another new powder, one that should prove very interesting: IMR8208XBR. Designed to be insensitive to temperature fluctuations, it has a burn rate slightly faster than IMR4895. It will work well in the smaller cases like the .223 Remington and .308 Winchester, as well as the large-bore magnums like the .458 Winchester Magnum. Famed writer and shooter Jim Carmichael used this powder to win the International Benchrest Shooters National Championship Heavy Varmint division, in 2009.

Alliant has recently developed some cutting edge powders. The aforementioned Reloder series is now made more versatile on the high and low end, with the inclusion of Reloder 25, designed for the overbored magnum cartridges like .30-378 Weatherby, .300 Remington Ultra Magnum, and their ilk, and Reloder 15, which is perfectly suited for medium burn rate cartridges like the .308 Winchester and .375 H&H Magnum. Reloder 7 is designed for the small varmint calibers, like the .22 Hornet and .222 Remington, but it also works very well in the larger straight-walled cartridges like the .45-70 Government, .458 Winchester Magnum, and .444 Marlin.

Alliant has some specialty powders for new cartridges, too. Reloder 17 is a perfect fit for the Winchester lineup of WSM cartridges, and Reloder 33 is designed to perform in the long-range .338 Lapua case. The Alliant Power Pro series of powders changed up its configuration from stick to spherical, and the new 4000-MR has given very good results in our 7mm Remington Magnums and .300 Winchester Magnums. I've also used it in the .270 Winchester with great accuracy.

VihtaVuori is a powder company from Finland, whose products are gaining a solid reputation in the States. I had a good time experimenting with N550 in our .30-06 test rifle, achieving respectable velocities and accuracy. VihtaVuori has a complete lineup of powders in varying burn rates, making them suitable for reloading nearly any of your favorite cartridges.

Accurate Arms Powders is another company delivering great powders. It offers a full range of burn rates, from fast pistol powders up to and including the company's MagPro, which is designed for the Winchester WSM series and the Remington SAUM line. I haven't loaded an awful lot of Accurate's powders, but I have friends who swear by it, and I have no reason whatsoever to doubt their data. Accurate's sister company, Ramshot, has some great powders being made in Belgium. Big Game, Magnum, and Terminator powders will fill a wide variety of rifle cases, while the True Blue and Silhouette are good pistol powders.

Hodgdon has introduced an entire line of "Extreme Extruded Powders" for rifles. They are cut in grain lengths that will flow well through the variety of today's many powder measuring devices, and these powders also show insensitivity to temperature fluctuations. The powders H322, Varget, Retumbo, and H4831SC are all part of this series. Consistency being the key to accuracy, the minimal variations in these powders makes them a very good choice. They are designed to be less affected by temperature variations and, therefore, give a more uniform velocity, regardless whether you're shooting in Texas or Manitoba.

Hodgdon's TiteGroup is a newer powder, one designed for a wide range of pistol cartridges. Its purpose is to obtain standard velocity with less powder than would normally be anticipated with an older powder style. It does just that and is very accurate!

While chatting with Chris Hodgdon about some of the new developments coming along, he was very excited about a new powder called

Hodgdon's TiteGroup will work in most common pistol calibers.

CFE223. The "CFE" portion stands for "Copper Fouling Eraser" and, according to Chris, this powder actually removes a good portion of the copper fouling in your bore as you shoot. It was designed to have a burn rate a bit slower than IMR4064 or Varget and it works fine in any cartridge that will handle a medium burn rate powder. Chris explained it was named for the .223 Remington, and that round is indeed a great application for this powder. A CFE pistol powder will also be unveiled soon. Exciting stuff, especially if it does in fact make the chore of cleaning an easier prospect!

BRASS

Component brass is being made by more companies than ever before. It used to be the case that you would save your empty factory brass for reloading, as the manufacturers of new component brass were few and far between. Things have certainly changed, and brass makers now make up their own little industry, pandering to us handloaders. This is good.

The major ammunition manufacturers were among the first to offer new brass to the handloader, and now we have a wide array of choices to fill our needs. Remington still produces brass with the "R-P" headstamp, harking back to the Remington-Peters days. Remington brass has to be among my absolute favorite to load. It gives great accuracy and great longevity, these cases capable of being reloaded many times. Winchester still makes component brass, but, instead of the "Super-X" or "W-W Super"

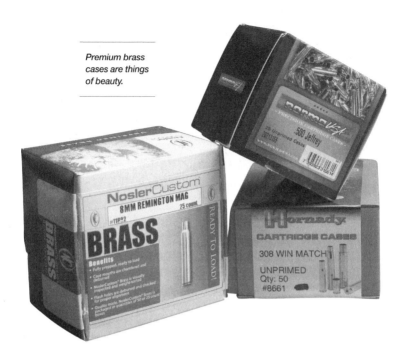

Premium brass cases are things of beauty.

Early Remington component brass, this being the venerable speedster .220 Swift.

headstamp of years ago, it now simply reads "Winchester" or "Win." These cases are, as they always have been, quality component cases. The Federal Cartridge Company continues to produce its great brass, and it is a favorite of many shooters, myself included.

The big three companies more than likely comprise the majority of the brass that is on hand today, and for good reason: All three companies make a good product in a wide selection of both pistol and rifle brass and in all the common calibers available today. A good percentage of it is also available as nickel-plated brass, which is resistant to tarnishing. The brass produced by these companies is often sold in bulk bags and must be properly sized (and sometimes trimmed) before being loaded. The

Modern Remington cases.

.300 Winchester cases with Winchester's "W-W Super" headstamp.

case mouths are often slightly dented or out of round, a hazard of shipping in bulk bags. A quick trip through the resizing die and a good inner and outer neck chamfer will get the brass right into shape and ready to be loaded. These cases are usually very uniform and can produce some great shooting ammunition.

Some of the major bullet manufacturers have hopped onto the brass case train. Nosler produces its own line of rifle brass, now, and it is wonderful stuff. The cases are held to very tight tolerances and sorted out by weight. Flash holes are checked for proper alignment and all burrs are removed. The case mouths are chamfered inside and out, so these cases are ready to be primed and loaded right out of the box. They are a bit more expensive, but they are well worth it. Nosler offers its brass in many of the common calibers, as well as some of the hard-to-find rarities such as the .264 Winchester Magnum, 8mm Remington Magnum, and even the .280 Remington Ackley Improved (with a 40-degree shoulder). I'm a big fan of Nosler brass.

Hornady threw its hat in the component brass ring years ago with its Frontier line of brass and ammunition, which was good stuff. It is now marketed with the Hornady headstamp, and the cases are good-quality, very consistent cases. Hornady is the best source of cases for the Ruger line of cartridges, including the RCM (Ruger Compact Magnum), and the .375 Ruger and .416 Ruger cartridges so popular in gun maker's Hawkeye rifle series. Hornady also produces affordable brass for large classic double rifles, such as the .450-400 3-inch and

(Photos both pages courtesy Massaro Media Group & J.D. Fielding Photography)

Nosler Custom brass is among the finest available. These 8mm Remington Magnum cases are increasingly hard to find, but Nosler provides component brass for many such rarities.

the .500 Nitro Express. I really like the way the Hornady .416 Rigby brass shoots out of my CZ550 rifle. Hornady also produces good pistol brass, mainly for the larger pistol rounds like my favorite .45 Colt, the big .454 Casull, and the bigger yet .460 S&W. Working in conjunction with Sturm, Ruger & Co., Hornady helped to develop the big, honkin' .480 Ruger pistol round and make available component brass for this cartridge, as well. It has also worked with the Marlin Company to help develop the .308 Marlin Express and the .338 Marlin Express, which help to improve the ballistics of the classic lever-action gun. Hornady is a great source for the brass for these cartridges.

In addition to the variety already noted, Hornady produces a line of Match Brass in .308 Winchester and

the behemoth .50 BMG. I haven't had the opportunity to load and shoot Mr. Browning's beast in Hornady form, but I can certainly attest to the quality of the Hornady .308 Match cases. I loaded them with IMR4064 and a Federal Gold Medal Match primer, launching 150-grain Swift Scirocco II bullets to print 100-yard three-shot groups that average between 0.3-inch and 0.25-inch from my Suzie Q's 20-inch barreled Savage bolt-action rifle. You really can't ask any more than that from an out-of-the-box hunting rifle and a 3-9x scope!

Norma, of Sweden, has produced great component brass for years. Strict uniformity, along with annealed case necks, make for a long-lasting product that will serve you well for years. More often than not, Norma cases come ready to load out of the box. As a habit, I usu-

Hornady brass cases.

The beastly .338 Lapua, a long-range affair par excellence.

(Photo courtesy Massaro Media Group & J.D. Fielding Photography)

High-quality Norma brass is a loader's dream!

ally run the necks over the expander ball of the resizing die just to give the best concentricity, and I give them a quick inside and outside chamfering, but that's about it. Norma cases have given me stellar accuracy in both my .22-250 Rem. and my .300 Winchester Magnum. I had a friend's .243 Winchester that went from goat to hero, just by changing his brass to Norma's.

Lapua, originating from Finland, is also a producer of premium brass cases. The firm is famous for its long-range powerhouse .338 Lapua Magnum, which is well-loved by military snipers and benchrest shooters alike. Lapua offers brass for most, but not all, the popular rifle calibers. Its lineup includes some rarities that can be used as the parent case for many wildcats. For example, the .220 Russian case is able to be made into the .22 PPC and 6mm PPC, and the .221 Fireball is a great base case for the .300 AAC Blackout cartridge. The Lapua .308 Winchester cases are an excellent means of making that already inherently accurate cartridge really shine, and the .30-06 brass from Lapua can wring that last bit of accuracy out of your old, favorite, big-game rifle. Lapua also manufactures handgun brass for the .32 S&W Long and the ever-popular 9mm Luger pistols. All Lapua brass has proven to me to be of the best quality available. If you're a serious accuracy hound, you really can't go wrong in choosing Lapua brass for your load development.

Lapua cases. Very high-quality stuff.

Starline makes only pistol brass, but it is among the best. The headstamp features a clever *-* on the rim. My .45 Colt revolver shoots very well with Starline brass and, frankly, regardless the caliber, I've never had a bad experience with it. Not an awful lot to discuss, just a continuously dependable product. I recommend it for the handgun hunter who wants a higher level of accuracy.

Lake City brass is of military origin and offered for sale by many of the major reloading retailers. It's great way to feed your .308 (or 7.62mm NATO) or your .223 (5.56mm NATO). Being designed for military use, the case walls are often thicker than the sporting variety, so either use load data developed for that thicker military brass or reduce the loads as recommended in the reloading manuals. Here's the thought process behind this practice: The cartridge *outside* dimensions must adhere to the SAAMI specifications, so a thicker case will result in a smaller *inside* dimension (capacity) and, therefore, a smaller combustion chamber. Pressures will rise higher and at a faster rate in thick-walled military cases, given the same loading for a non-military case. You must be sure to sort any military brass into a separate lot, so that it may be loaded correctly.

MagTech makes a great lineup of handgun cases for both pistols and revolvers, in addition to military rifle brass. Brass for the .223 Rem., .308 Winchester, .30 M1 Carbine, and .50 BMG are all available unprimed.

When you shoot a rifle that is chambered for a "proprietary" round (one that is not chambered by any other company than the one that developed it), the availability of ammunition and brass is limited. Components, therefore, are precious. Weatherby was in this category for a long while. The Weatherby-brand brass and ammunition has always been produced by Norma, and though other companies produce ammunition and components for Weatherby calibers, if you want that Weatherby headstamp, Weatherby is the one to offer it in component form. (Components for some of the less-popular Weatherby calibers are produced for Weatherby through Norma alone.) Lazzeroni is another propriety cartridge company that produce its own brass cases for its unique cartridges. As far as I know, no other company makes cases for the Lazzeroni calibers. The same holds true for Dakota lineup of cartridges. The 7mm Dakota and .300 Dakota are probably the most popular among these chamberings, but you'll have to invest in Dakota brass if you choose to shoot these cartridges. Brass from any of these makers is of good quality and just as capable of having a long reloading life as that from other makers, if properly taken care of.

The Hornady Lock-N-Load Classic press.

RELOADING PRESSES

For years, I only had access to one press: my dad's Lee Turret press. He bought it when I was an infant, and he later taught me how to load on it. It is still in his possession, and it still works fine. It doesn't hold the tightest tolerances in the world, but, if I could pile up the cartridges it has produced, your head might spin! It's made rounds for three African safaris for yours truly, not to mention numerous hunts across North America and the thousands of rounds spent in practice

and load development for my many rifles, not to mention all the loading that press did for friends and relatives! That says a ton for the durability of this product.

I graduated to a pair of RCBS presses once I set up my own bench. Both the Rockchucker and Rockchucker II still sit on my bench, along with some others. The RCBS Rockchucker was and is the industry standard, in my opinion. It is a simple design, with a cast iron "O"-shaped

The classic RCBS Rock Chucker, a press that still sits proudly on the bench at Massaro Ballistic Laboratories!

frame and a steel ram. It is a single-stage press, holding only one reloading die at a time, and this simple design is the beauty. It can produce very good ammunition with very tight tolerances, and the press is built ruggedly enough to last a lifetime or more. There are many designs like it, such as the Lyman Orange Crusher 2 and the Redding Big Boss. With all of them, heavy, durable frames, sound-fitting hinges and pins, and the ability to prime cases on the press all add up to a great value for the loader. For my single-stage work, I like this design. The cast iron frame gives enough rigidity to ensure tight tolerances, and the steel ram withstands the leverage needed for camming-over brass cases to resize them properly.

Hornady offers the Lock-N-load press with a cast alloy frame offset at 30 degrees for ease of access to the case. Lee makes two similar presses, one called the Challenger Breech Lock, the other the Classic Cast. The Challenger is made from solid aluminum, while the Classic Cast is of cast iron. All three come with a built-in priming tool, and the Breech Lock has a quick-change die system that allows you to easily swap out dies without unscrewing them.

In addition to its classic Rock Chucker Series, RCBS has developed some new models in the "O"-style design. The Reloader Special 5 is built with tall rods connecting the top and bottom of the press, an arrangement that provides enough space to load the .50 BMG cartridge and everything smaller. The RCBS

Partner is an inexpensive, entry-level press constructed of a cast aluminum frame. While not as strong as cast iron, it is a good press for those just getting into reloading and is offered for sale as a kit containing almost all the other necessary equipment you need.

RCBS also has a revolutionary new press on the market, the Summit. This press changes the entire mechanical idea of the classic reloading press by moving the reloading dies on a large, two-inch diameter ram downward over the case, rather than the ram raising the case into the die. It has a handle that's able to be moved to either side of the press for right- or left-hand use, and its massive ram has a built-in grease fitting to keep it well lubricated. It obtains great leverage, and if I had to find one fault with the press it is that it doesn't have a priming attachment. You must prime your cases with a hand primer. All said, I've really grown to like this press and use it often.

Redding Reloading has long been known as a producer of rock-solid loading equipment. The Big Boss press I've mentioned is one example, the Ultra Mag press another. A large, cast iron "C"-frame press, this beast can easily handle the longest cartridges. The location of the linkage attachment at the top portion of the press takes away the possibility of press flexure, and the wide space available makes loading the big Sharps-style cases like the .45-110 and .45-120, as well as Nitro-Express cases like the .450 NE and .500 NE,

The RCBS Summit press, an entirely new idea in press design.

The Redding T7 Turret Press.

an easy proposition. Redding presses feature the company's Smart Primer Arm, which swings out of the way on the upstroke of the ram.

Forster has a really neat press called the Co-Ax, which uses two long rods to accurately guide the lower portion of the press up toward the area that holds the dies. In addition, the press doesn't use a threaded bushing to hold the dies. Instead, there's a slotted recess in the upper portion where the dies snap in. They're held in place by the lock ring, without requiring the die threads to come into

play. It is probably the fastest method of changing dies in any single-stage press. Forster has also removed the need for a shellholder, by creating a set of spring-loaded jaws that grab the shell by the recessed cannelure at the shell's base. This allows the press to grab a shell of just about any design and helps to precisely center the cartridge. I can attest to the level of precision and accuracy this press can produce; some .308 Winchester ammunition made on a Forster shoots in the realm of ¼-MOA, repeatedly.

Turret presses are a great aid to

the pistol reloader, and even the rifle reloader, because the die holder can hold three, four, or even seven dies or accessories at once. Simply turn the turret on the top of the press and you have a resizing die, a flaring die, or seating die. There is little to no need to screw in and unscrew dies. The Lee Classic turret press I mentioned earlier has served me and my dad very well, making both pistol and rifle cartridges with relative ease. Lee still produces it, and it is a good value for the budget-minded reloader who doesn't want to shell out for a progressive.

Redding makes the T-7 turret press and, like most of its products, it is a solid piece of gear. In addition to cast iron construction, a seven-hole turret, and the ability to automatically feed primers, this press features compound leverage and the same Smart Primer arm as the Big Boss and the UltraMag presses. It has plenty of clearance for long rifle cartridges.

The Lyman T-Mag II is also a well-made turret press. It features a six-hole removable turret for ease of caliber change, as well as a turret handle for both turning the turret quickly and removing the turret itself. The T-Mag II comes with a priming arm and spent primer catcher, as well.

Dillon Precision has a turret-style press called the BL550 and, like most of Dillon's products, it's a winner. It can be used as single-stage type press, with the benefits of the turret capability, or upgraded to an auto-priming and powder-dispensing behemoth that can crank out vast quanti-

ties of very good ammunition, nearly along the lines of a progressive.

Speaking of progressive presses, these can be the pistol cartridge reloader's best friend. Such a press performs multiple functions every time you pull on the handle, working with a rotating plate that will move the case from station to station.

Progressive presses are set up to work in this order: Station 1 will deprime and resize in the resizing die; many will re-prime on the upstroke, as an automatic primer feeder delivers the new primer from underneath. Station 2 will flare the case mouth of the pistol cartridge. Station 3 is a case-activated powder dispenser, fully adjustable so as to deliver a proper powder charge. (I still advise that you check it often against your scale, especially when loading the smaller pistol cartridges, where a half-grain of excess powder can cause excessive and dangerous pressures.) Station 4 seats the bullet and, depending on whether you choose to use a separate crimping die, may crimp on the same stroke. Station 5 can be your separate crimping stroke. Once everything is set up properly, five strokes on the handle should give you a properly loaded cartridge, with a new one on every pull thereafter.

Progressives are produced by most of the major reloading companies. The RCBS Pro2000 Auto Index is a well-made piece of gear, with a cast iron frame and a five-station top. It comes with the RCBS Uniflow powder measure (which has a stellar reputation), and a removable die plate. That's a convenient feature if you load more than one caliber, as you can leave the dies all set up on a plate and simply swap it for the one in the press as needed. Shellholder plates are sold separately, but the priming strips are included. The only issue I have with this press is that the plastic primer strips can gum up the works if they are not perfectly aligned, and then it's a pain in the proverbial arse to get the piece of plastic out of the machine. Priming issues aside, it's a damned good machine. I also understand there's a metal tube priming system available for conversion, but I haven't as yet looked into replacing the primer strips on my own press. Being an auto-indexing machine (the raising and lowering of the ram turns the shell plate counter-clockwise), you must work the ram fully each time, so that the same amount of powder is dispensed and the shells are equally resized, flared, etc., in each of those respective stations.

Hornady sells the Lock-N-load AP progressive press, which has many features similar to those of the Pro2000 from RCBS. Made with a cast alloy frame, it has a slightly different indexing mechanism, moving halfway to the next station on the downstroke and halfway on the upstroke. Hornady offers a die bushing system that allows for quicker changes of dies. Once you get your dies properly set up, you simply release the bushings and switch the dies.

The RCBS
Pro2000
Auto Index
progressive
press.

Lee Precision makes products that are among the most affordable, if not the fanciest. Its progressive presses are a good value; Lee offers two models aimed at the high-volume reloader. The Lee Pro 1000 press is designed to load handgun cartridges. It has a three-hole top similar to those on turret presses, a ProDisk powder dispenser, and an automatic primer feeder. Cartridges can be loaded one at a time for fine adjustment, and the primer will feed only if a case is present at that station. Lee warns that only Remington or CCI primers will function properly through the priming system. To use other brands, you must purchase the "explosion shield." Um, not for nothing, I'd personally stick with the Remington or CCI primers. I'm not a fan of words like "explosion shield." Maybe it's just me.

The Lee Loadmaster progressive can handle either rifle or pistol cases. It has a five-hole top that can be removed or replaced (for multiple die sets), a bigger steel frame, and a cast aluminum handle. It's a good press for the money. The Loadmaster and Pro 1000 can be purchased as kits, complete with the appropriate die set and shellplate necessary for the caliber chosen.

Dillon Precision Products makes the Cadillac of progressive handgun presses. The XL650 is a no-nonsense, five-station progressive to which you manually feed the cases and bullets. The cases are fed mouth up into a tube that sets them into the shellholder. The frame is huge, so flexure is never an issue. The powder dispenser is case-activated, so there's no chance of powder spilling all over the bench. Overall operation isn't all that much different than with any other progressive, but the add-ons are wonderful. There's an electronic case feeder that automatically places

the cases mouth up into the feed tube, and a powder check device assures you don't double charge or forget to charge a case. If it detects a significant change in powder level, an alarm goes off to warn you and prevent a possible tragedy.

The Dillon Square-Deal B has a unique square-shaped ram, machined brass link arm bearings, and a smaller rotating shell holder. The primer feed operates on a slide, and the finished cartridge is ejected down a chute into a hopper. Both presses come with a full set of tools to adjust things, and Dillon offers a lifetime warranty, whether you purchased the press new or used. I've yet to meet a reloader who hasn't been thrilled with Dillon products.

Whichever brand of progressive press you choose, be sure and do an awful lot of homework before you invest your money. Make sure that a press' operation isn't too complicated for what you're after. In fact, I recommend watching as many tutorial videos as possible on all the different makes and models. Seeing the press you want in action can be very valuable. Many reloading forums, too, will have some brutally honest reviews and helpful hints to make life easier with such machines.

RELOADING DIES

These pieces of machined brilliance are the unsung heroes of the reloading process. They get little or none of the glory, but can and will make or break your day. Quality dies set up properly in a good press

Dies for the .33 Winchester, made by Pacific, a predecessor of Hornady reloading dies. Old is not dead. These give good service.

are the ticket to accuracy. Misaligned dies or inferior quality dies will make ammunition that won't fit your gun at worst, or won't shoot well at best.

Older dies, if well cared for, are just fine to use. I have an old set of Pacific dies for the obsolete .33 Winchester that I found for sale at a gun show. Pacific is long gone, but these dies looked new in the box and they work just fine. My Dad's dies, other than needing some cleaning, also still make great ammunition. Still, like most other components I've covered, reloading dies have made progress and benefitted from better technology.

Most if not all companies use a standard $7/8$-inch/14 thread on the die bodies, unless you bump up to the big safari calibers like the .450 Rigby and .500 Nitro Express. These bigger rounds use dies with a thread size of 1-inch/14, and you will need to buy an adapter bushing for your press to use these. The basic design of the re-sizing, flaring, and bullet seating dies haven't changed all that much, but I think there are some advancements that should be highlighted.

For the bolt-action fan, there are neck-sizing dies available for just about every bottlenecked cartridge. The advantage of the neck-sizing die is that the body of the case doesn't

Lee Carbide pistol dies, shown here in .45 ACP.

(Photos both pages courtesy Massaro Media Group & J.D. Fielding Photography)

become over-worked, thereby extending the life of your cases, plus the case is perfectly formed to the chamber of the rifle in which it was fired. The drawback is that it is rifle specific and can't be used in any other rifle of the same caliber. Redding, RCBS, Hornady, Lyman, and most others offer neck-sizing dies. It will be a bit more difficult to close the bolt on a neck-sized cartridge, but that usually comes with an increase in accuracy.

Carbide pistol dies are a wonderful advancement. The long and the short of these is that they don't require the cases to be lubricated. There's a carbide insert inside the pistol die, and it is much harder than traditional steel. These dies make the high-volume pistol loader's job much shorter. No sticky lubricant to apply or remove, just crank the cases through the resizing die. Again, most companies offer a carbide pistol die set.

Competition-style dies for rifle cartridges are definitely a worthwhile investment. The bullet seating dies have a micrometer adjustment on the top of the die that provides for precise seating depth. This allows complete control of cartridge overall length, and the spring-loaded micrometer holds adjustment much better than the traditional threaded rod style.

Redding competition dies rate among the best, and there are no flies on the RCBS or Forster models, either. Hornady offers a replacement seating stem for its Dimension seating dies, which convert a standard seating die into a micrometer-adjustable seater. Neat idea!

I came across a little reloading die company out of Georgia by the name of Whidden Gunworks. This company offers a micrometer-adjustable seating die with a floating bushing that not only allows precise seating depth, but also increases bullet concentricity. I like the way this up and coming company thinks!

Each brand of dies has its own unique features, and I'll do my best to briefly outline them here.

Hornady has some interesting die features. The first I like is the elliptical expander ball, in which the diameter of the ball grows as you raise the case into the die. The one place I find this most useful is during the creation of wildcat brass. For instance, the

.35 Whelen is nothing more than a .30-06 Springfield necked up to hold .358-inch diameter bullets, so, if you wanted to make some brass for your Whelen out of .30-06 brass, this expander ball will work the neck more slowly, thereby reducing stress. I like this feature, and Hornady sells it as a replacement part for RCBS-type dies.

Another Hornady feature I admire, though small it may be, is its lock ring. All lock rings have wrench flats, which aren't a bad thing, but the part I like about Hornady's is that the screw to lock the ring down doesn't fight against the die body threads. The ring is split, so the screw tightens the ring against itself. Because of this design, there's no risk of marring the die body threads if someone gets gorilla because the lock ring won't move.

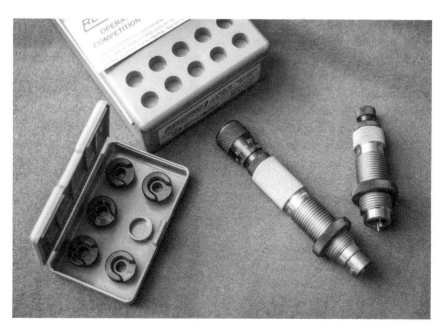

Redding .308 Winchester competition dies.

A Hornady three-die set, with split lock rings.

One feature I'm on the fence about is Hornady's floating bullet seater. It is designed to seat bullets more concentrically, because it rides on the case neck and the bullet. I've had good and bad experiences with it. The good times worked out just fine, but, with bullets that have a long ogive, I've had this rig leave an impressed ring around the bullet, about halfway down the ogive. Perhaps I had a set of dies that were out of adjustment for some reason, but it made me insane. When I loaded round-nosed bullets, there were no issues whatsoever.

Redding Reloading, from my home state of New York, makes some

Hornady dies, with a floating bullet seater.

(Photo courtesy Massaro Media Group & J.D. Fielding Photography)

of my favorite dies ever. The tolerances are very tight, the machine work is clean, and the structural integrity is about the best you'll find. Redding uses very good steel in its dies. The standard adjustment at the top of the dies are made of blued, knurled steel, and all the die sets are shipped with a spare decapping pin and a hex wrench for adjusting the lock rings. The lock rings are held in place by placing a piece of lead shot between the set screw and the die body, so the threads can't be boogered up. The inside of the dies are all polished to a bright sheen, ultrasonically cleaned, and coated in a rust preventative for shipping. The rust preventative must be removed with a solvent before using the dies, but that is a relatively simple process. I find Redding dies to be among the finest you can buy, and you won't be

sorry for choosing them. The plastic die box even doubles as a loading block, with recessed holes to hold the cartridges. When it comes to producing very accurate ammunition, Redding knows how to pay attention to fine details. The company also has a great customer service department, with folks more than willing to help and answer your questions.

RCBS has long been the industry standard for many reloading tools. It sort of set the benchmark, back in the day. Standard RCBS dies are a great value and, with proper care, should last you a lifetime. They are available in almost every caliber, from the teeny .17 Remington up to the big .500 Jeffrey and .505 Gibbs; the RCBS custom shop will go far beyond that. Die adjustments are held in place with a ¼-inch nut, and the set screw on the lock ring is made of

Redding dies are among the very best constructed reloading dies available.

(Photo courtesy Massaro Media Group & J.D. Fielding Photography)

brass so the die's body threads won't be mangled. Lock rings have wrench flats and, generally speaking, the de-priming pins are interchangeable. RCBS is a great source of forming dies that are used to convert brass from one case to another. If you have a firearm chambered for an obsolete cartridge and brass is impossible to come by but can be made from another case with common attributes, these dies can breathe new life into the that old gun.

Where applicable, RCBS offers two seater plugs for its seating dies, for loading either spitzer-point bullets or round-nosed bullets. This is a good investment if you load for both types of bullets, as it won't mar or crush the bullet meplat. RCBS also produces a series of X dies that are designed to stop the elongation of

brass cases during the sizing process by using a special mandrel inside the resizing die. This design limits the amount of brass that flows forward into the neck during sizing. While I haven't used these dies myself, I have friends who report that they do reduce the amount of brass flow, enough to almost eliminate the need to trim brass. I have found RCBS customer service to be impeccable.

Lyman has produced great reloading tools for many years, and its many tools have been relied upon by legions of shooters to make great ammo. Lyman Precision reloading dies are no exception to the company's solid reputation. Made of quality steel and well polished, they are available in most popular calibers, as well as in the blackpowder calibers of the late 1800s, like the .45-70, .45-

An RCBS rifle reloading die set, shown here for the .270 Winchester Short Magnum.

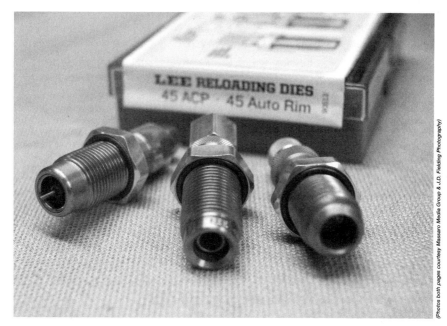

Lee pistol dies.

(Photos both pages courtesy Massaro Media Group & J.D. Fielding Photography)

90, .45-110, and .50-90. One product from Lyman I particularly enjoy is the Universal Decapping Die, as it has a hardened decapping pin and assembly that work perfectly for punching out the crimped-in primers in military brass.

Lee Precision offers a plethora of dies. They are made to be affordable, using a rubber gasket to lock down the dies in lieu of a set screw, aluminum lock rings in lieu of steel, etc. This affordability should not be construed as inferiority. Lee dies are very capable of producing quality ammunition. They are a great value, for each die set comes with a shellholder, powder scoop, and charge table of appropriate and suitable powder charges. I am a huge fan of the Lee Factory Crimp Die. It gives a roll or taper crimp (depending on ap-

plication) unlike any other, and I use it often, especially with my .45 ACP ammunition. It leaves the case mouth nice and square for proper headspacing, yet holds the bullet as snugly as if it were a babe at mother's bosom.

Dillon has some innovative features in both its pistol and rifle dies. The unique feature of the rifle dies that I enjoy is the placement of the expander ball. Instead of placing it at the bottom of the die near the shellholder, as many others do, it is higher in the die, where the leverage of the press is much stronger and can be better utilized. This allows for smoother expansion of the case neck. Dillon pistol dies feature a clip retainer on the top of the seating die, allowing you to change bullet seaters from round-nosed to semi-wadcutter or the like in a flash. Remove the clip, switch seaters, and your die is still perfectly adjusted for the case you're loading. I've seen these Dillon dies in action on the Dillon 550B progressive, and they work just fine.

POWDER MEASURERS

The ability to dispense powder in a quick and accurate manner is very helpful, especially to the shooter who needs to produce large quantities of ammunition. I'm old fashioned, and often I still scoop powder by hand when making rifle loads that are destined for the hunting fields or for accuracy testing from the bench. However, the IDPA pistol shooter or a shooter who wants to shoot 3-Gun competition wants large quantities of ammunition that might not possess hair-splitting accuracy, but will suffice for the job at hand. A powder measure can certainly speed the loading process along, and the powder measures of today are capable of dropping a very precise charge. Most are threaded to fit the $7/8$-inch/14 threads needed to mount on a reloading press.

The basic construction of the powder measure hasn't really changed over the years, but its overall construction and accuracy has. Now, I've never shot in a formal, officiated benchrest competition, so I was shocked to find out that the serious benchrest folks don't weigh their charges, rather they measure by volume from a powder measure. Why? The large plastic hopper that holds the powder is still the same as it was in yesteryear, but the adjustment mechanisms

have come leaps and bounds.

Redding leads the field in ultra-accurate powder dispensers, in my opinion. Machine work on the moving parts is held to extreme tolerances, and Redding has different models to cover a variety of loading needs. The powder charge adjustment has a high-quality micrometer that won't suffer backlash or come out of adjustment. The Model 3BR is a flexible unit, with two chambers available. The pistol chamber throws between one and 10 grains, and the universal chamber throws between five and 100 grains. The Bench Rest model, the BR-30, throws 10 to 50 grains and was designed to work well for large-capacity handgun cases and medium-sized rifles cases. The Competition Model 10X is formatted around pistol and small rifle volume capacities, those between one and 25 grains, while the LR1000 is designed for the large magnum rifle cases like the .416 Rigby and .338 Lapua, this model being capable of throwing up to 140 grains of powder. Redding's Robin Sharpless and I had a great conversation about powder measures, and he indicated to me that the best and most accurate results occur in the middle third of the capacity of the measure. You can see that Redding offers a measure for just about every application, so you won't be stretching the limits of the capacity.

RCBS still produces the venerable UniFlow powder measure, and it's as good as it ever was. It has large and small micrometer adjustment screws, for use with different size chambers, and throughout the range of the two

Redding's powder measure.

can throw up to 50 grains of powder. It is threaded to be used in a reloading press. The RCBS Competition powder measure has a micrometer adjustment (unlike the UniFlow), which can be used to accurately observe the setting for your powder charge of choice and reproduce the load to save time in the setup of the powder measure. The RCBS Quick Change measure gives the most flexibility in the line; with the pull of a pin and a change of the metering assembly, you can load light pistol loads one minute and heavy magnum rifle loads the next.

Lyman offers the No. 55 powder measure, which measures up to 200 grains of powder, and Lee has its Perfect Powder Measure that displays the volume in cubic centimeters. Hornady has a powder measure in its Lock-N-Load series of reloading tools, with a broad range of 0.5 to 75 grains of powder.

Whichever measure you choose, look carefully and be sure it will dispense powder in the range of weights you intend to load. Keep your measure clean and well lubricated and it should give you many years of good results.

ELECTRONIC POWDER DISPENSERS

I don't easily leave the path of traditional reloading gear. Such tools were the ones I was taught with, they worked for me, and, so, I saw no real reason to change it. One piece of gear has brought me around, though, and that's the electronic powder dispenser. These are simple, really. A motor-driven powder dispenser dumps a specific powder charge (measured down to 0.1-grain) into the pan of an electronic scale. My buddy Mark "Pig Newton" Nazi sang its praises, and Mark is a loader whose opinion I respect. Still, being a traditionalist, I didn't buy into the idea until I tried it. Well, it worked so well that not only could I not find fault with it, I went out and got one for myself. I picked up the same one Mark had, the RCBS Charge Master 1500, and gave it a workout.

Simple to assemble, I zeroed the scale, added my powder of choice, punched in the desired charge weight, and *voilá*! I checked the charges thrown on my trusty ol' beam scale, and they were spot on. I know digital scales have a reputation for drifting from zero and are supposedly affected by barometric pressure, but I haven't had a charge thrown that didn't measure properly on a beam scale. I do zero the electronic scale often, but the loads are very consistent. I love the feature that automatically dispenses another charge once you've replaced the pan and the scale reads zero, plus the fact that the display even gives the count of the loads dispensed (a good way to double-check how many cases you think you've filled, if you're filling many cases as a group before moving on to bullet seating). The machine is capable of storing your favorite load weights for recall the next time you load, and, if a charge is thrown more than 0.1-grain on the heavy side, an audible alarm notifies you. The only warning I could give you about this tool is to make certain you close the

The RCBS ChargeMaster 1500 electronic scale and powder dispenser.

(Photo courtesy Massaro Media Group & J.D. Fielding Photography)

little rotary port that drains the powder out of the reservoir. If you don't, you'll dump powder all over your bench, just like I did!

RCBS isn't the only company making this type of rig. Lyman makes its GEN5 and GEN6 models and,

if they're made as well as the older Lyman models, the company has two winners. My pal Steve Darling has an older model Lyman electric dispenser that gives great results. Hornady has a Lock-N-Load electronic dispenser complete with all the bells and

The digital display and powder pan of the ChargeMaster 1500.

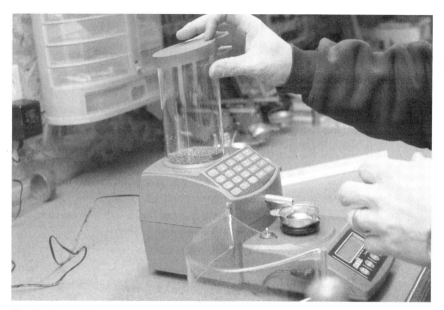

The plastic powder hopper.

whistles you might want, like speed adjustment, a large display, and more.

The speed of these machines is a huge time-saver, as long as you keep an eye on things like the electronic scale and weigh the charges on your beam scale every so often. Just one little note about the manual and electronic dispensers that use a plastic hopper to store powder (and that pretty much includes all models I'm aware of). I've read numerous reviews and comments about certain types of powder "melting" to the plastic if left in the hopper for long periods of time.

I've never had it happen to me, but I've seen photos, so I'd recommend that you empty the hopper immediately after you conclude your loading session. Better to be safe than sorry!

Oh, and, one more thing: *Never* use a powder dispenser to measure blackpowder. Never! These dispensers are capable of producing static electricity, which will very easily ignite black powder. These tools are designed for smokeless powder only, and there are special tools out there for measuring blackpowder, which feature no plastic parts.

CHAPTER 7

THE RIGHT COMBINATION FOR THE JOB

A tight group from the .338 Winchester Magnum, less than one MOA!

(Photos both pages courtesy Massaro Media Group & J.D. Fielding Photography)

With the wide variety of powder companies and powder shapes and powder burn rates, combined with what is likely a larger variety of projectile shapes and sizes and construction, what do you do with it all? Well, dear reader, you pick up several reloading manuals and you read the ink off the pages. Not every manual tests a particular bullet weight/cartridge combination with every single available powder suitable for it, so only through diligent studying will you gain a thorough knowledge of powders that have a burn rate appropriate for your intended use. As a handloader, you owe it to yourself to build up your loads safely, so as not to exceed pressure limits. We are all after the same end result: To deliver the bullet to the target accurately and consistently, whether that target is a paper bull's-eye target or the game animal of your dreams.

There is a lot of fun in the quest for your own custom load, and during the processes you'll meet many people and make some great friends who enjoy handloading as much as you do. One thing is for certain: once you achieve a level of accuracy you haven't experienced before and the sense of pride when you shoot that sweetheart of a rifle you've loaded for, you'll never look at factory ammunition in the same light!

LOADING FOR THE HUNT

The benchrest shooter who aims only at paper targets isn't often concerned with the structural integrity of the projectile, so long as it delivers the accuracy they're longing for. Hunters, on the other hand, have a second part to the equation, and that is how a chosen bullet will perform once it's been delivered to the target. Will it over- or under-penetrate? Will it quickly and humanely dispatch the game animal? Will it unnecessarily destroy the meat or pelt? Is the cartridge chosen suitable for delivering the proper amount of killing energy on the game animal at the distances anticipated? I will briefly touch upon these points, as entire

careers have been made (or broken) debating them.

As a comparison, target shooters want the most consistent and accurate product available. Bullet weight should be held to very tight tolerances, usually in a configuration conducive to long-range accuracy. The long, sleek, hollowpoint bullets reign supreme in this realm. Berger VLDs and Sierra MatchKings quickly come to mind, as favorite choices. Both have a long ogive (or curved nose section), and feature a boat-tail design. This aids in minimizing the affects of wind drift and drag for better trajectory.

The true target bullet does not take into account the ability to kill game, for that is not its intended purpose. Rather, they are made to fly truer than true, with repeatable results. Often the bullets themselves are (or should be) weighed, to hold tolerances even tighter, as are the cartridge cases. These cases are hand trimmed to a precisely uniform length, using the best brass money can buy. Match grade primers get the nod, and all powder charges are weighed on a scale. This will yield the best results. The powder charge and type is experimented with, (adhering to the safe guidelines of the loading manual, of course), until the most accurate results are found; variations of as little as a tenth of a grain of powder can produce appreciable differences in accuracy. This often requires an awful lot of time at the bench, and once that "magic" load is found, it is guarded like a beautiful girlfriend at a nightclub. Copious amounts of notes are kept, regarding weather conditions at the range, pressure signs, seating

The Hornady GMX is a stoutly constructed bullet, one capable of good accuracy and neatly dispatching game animals, as evidenced by its fine ability to mushroom.

depth, accuracy, etc. Many times, the benchrest shooter will end up with three or four different loadings for a particular rifle, using different brands or weights of bullets.

One of the major differences in the ammunition I produce at Massaro Ballistic Laboratories is that I treat all my clients' hunting rounds in the same manner I would treat benchrest target rounds, and that makes a big difference in the performance of their hunting rifles. It also imparts an awful lot of confidence to the hunter, when the shot presents itself. Of course, the hunter must take into account the structure and strength of their chosen bullet and determine if it's proper for the intended quarry. This is sometimes

a complicated task. In spite of all the wonderful scopes, rifles, camouflage patterns, bullets, boots, and knives available, our goal as hunters has remained the same from time immemorial: to quickly and cleanly dispatch the game animal we are pursuing.

As rifle and pistol shooters, the bullet and only the bullet is the single part of the equation that touches the animal. As handloaders, we can and should tailor the bullet and cartridge to the job. I will offer the following as a loose guide to choosing the caliber/bullet combination for different hunting scenarios. Please don't send hate mail if you have a different combination that works well for you. I understand that everyone has their favorite

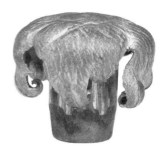

setup and, with sensible parameters, there's no wrong answer. Still, I make my living assembling handmade cartridges, and much of my work is for hunters pursuing dangerous game in Africa. Since the lives of those hunters depends, in large part, on what their bullets do when they make contact with something higher on the food chain than them, what I have to say should at least carry some weight.

For the varmint hunter, two types of bullets are predominant. The extremely frangible hollowpoint will decimate prairie dogs, woodchucks, and ground squirrels. Made to break apart easily, they offer up a whole bunch of hydraulic shock to create the famous "red mist," which generally means a fairly

instantaneous kill. Speer TNTs, Berger VLDs, and Nosler Ballistic Tips are all good choices for this kind of hunting. The second type of varmint bullet, one popular with serious varmint hunters who pursue the furbearers, is the full metal jacket. These provide almost no expansion whatsoever, so as to poke a caliber-sized hole through the animal and best preserve the pelt.

The most popular varmint calibers run from the .17 Remington up though the .25-caliber bores. Some folks enjoy using their favorite deer rifle for varmints and, with proper bullets, that combination can work just fine. Usually, varmint hunters like a flat-shooting cartridge, as prairie dogs and coyotes can present distant shots. Be

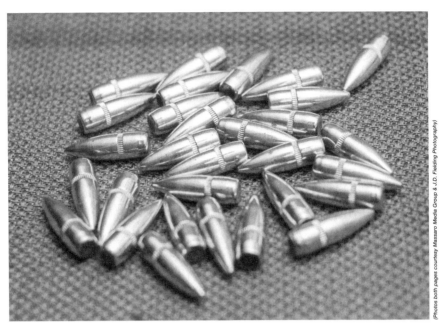

Winchester .224-inch 55-grain FMJs can be a useful tool for the varmint hunter who wants to preserve the pelts.

(Photos both pages courtesy Massaro Media Group & J.D. Fielding Photography)

cautious developing your handloads, watching for pressure signs, as you try to eke the most velocity you can from your chosen varmint caliber. A boat-tail bullet can help buck the wind, especially with lighter caliber bullets, which are more affected by wind drift. These loads often require a higher level of accuracy, in order to reliably connect on the smaller targets that varmints present.

I spent quite a bit of time developing loads for my own .22-250 Remington, using Hodgdon's H380 powder and 53-grain Sierra HP MatchKing bullets, until it printed three-shot groups of $^3/_8$-inch. My rifle has a sporter-weight barrel, so it heats up faster than the bull barrel so common among varmint rifles. My dad likes a full-pipe bolt-action .223 Remington, which shoots similar groups using Hodgdon's H335 backing the same bullet I use in the .22-250, though at a slightly lower velocity. Our friend Col. Le Frogg is a proponent of the .17 Remington, and he shoots the diminutive cartridge very well. The tiny 25- and 30-grain Berger hollowpoints at almost 4,000 fps certainly create the red mist, and pelt damage is minimal. In windy conditions, he favors a .25-06 with 87-grain bullets.

Whitetail deer, mule deer, and pronghorn antelope-sized game can be and often are taken with a wide range of cartridges and all sorts of bullets. In the South, where deer tend to be smaller, the .22 and 6mm calibers are very popular. These cartridges are also often the first rifle of young shooters, because of the low level of recoil. When it comes to hunting deer-sized game, based on my own experiences, I think these cartridges are best reserved for the well-seasoned rifleman who will wait for the perfect broadside shot. I also feel that a rifle in a .25-caliber through the .270 bore, loaded down to reduce recoil, is a better choice for the beginner, as they offer a heavier bullet. Still, if the .22 or 6mm is your choice, I feel it would be wise to take advantage of the newer developments in bullet technology and use a premium mono-metal or bonded-core bullet to make sure the bullet reaches the animal's vitals without premature breakup. For longer shots, say out beyond 250 yards, the light bullets made for these calibers can be more drastically affected by the wind, so, if such conditions are what you anticipate, try and choose a bullet to build your handloads around that will best buck the wind and help you hit your target.

The deer and antelope cartridges that make the most sense to me are between .257-inch and .308-inch in diameter. Each of the calibers offers mild, medium, spicy, and raucous cartridges. Historically, the .250 Savage, 7x57mm Mauser, .30-30 Winchester, and .308 Winchester have earned great reputations for being "easy shooters." They bring to the table a classic blend of killing power, accuracy, and low recoil. All (with the exception of the relatively slow .30-30), can be used to 300-plus yards by an experienced shooter who has familiarized themselves with the rifle and load, yet none should cause the dreaded flinch. These all have become classic deer calibers, in no small part because a standard cup-and-core bullet performs very well at their moderate velocities.

Stepping things up a bit, the .25-06, .270 Winchester, .280 Remington, and .30-06 Springfield all have a larger case, which equates to more powder capacity and, therefore, higher velocities. This higher velocity creates three things: more energy, flatter trajectory, and more recoil. Speeds in these rounds have not yet reached the point where bullet breakup is a problem, but the use of a premium bullet is not a ridiculous prospect. For all-around use, this class of cartridge makes an

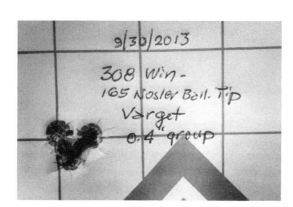

The sweet-shooting .308 Winchester is known for its accuracy.

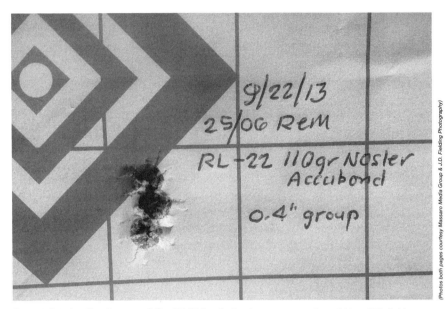

A great, flat-shooting deer round, the .25-06 Remington is a very accurate cartridge. This tight group was delivered from a Tikka T3 rifle.

awful lot of sense. You can choose the bullet diameter you like best, and there's probably going to be a case based on the .30-06 for you. I've never been on a hunt where the use of the .30-06 Springfield has been frowned upon, if any .30-caliber was deemed suitable for the intended game. There's nothing wrong with Jack O'Connor's pet .270 Winchester, either, and, with the bullets available today, I'm certain he'd be grinning like a Cheshire cat. Performance on game has dramatically increased with this round, thanks to the availability of projectiles that will stay together once fur is breached.

Crank it up another notch to the .257 Weatherby Magnum, .264 Winchester Magnum, .270 WSM, 7mm Remington Magnum, and my favorite, the .300 Winchester Magnum, and velocities increase 200 to 350 feet per second. Powder consumption also increases by 30 to 40 percent or so. This is where the use of standard cup-and-core bullets can make a mess on deer-sized game, when used up close at full-house velocities. Truly, these cases call for the premium bullet. Magnum primers are usually required to ignite the large powder charges.

When it comes to long-range shooting, the rounds in this last-mentioned class are my favorite balance of flat trajectory and acceptable recoil. Yes, in the Northeast deer and bear woods where I live, a case of this capacity is usually unwarranted. The lighter cases already mentioned will do the job, when shots are within 200 yards. But, follow my thinking for a second: As a handloader, I can safely and effectively reduce the velocity of my Winchester Model 70 in .300

These .300 Winchester Magnum cartridges were loaded with the 180-grain Swift Scirocco II, a bullet tough enough to easily withstand the high velocities the case is able to produce.

Winchester Magnum (that fits me like a glove) to perform like a .308 Winchester or .30-06 Springfield. I cannot do the same in reverse with either of those latter two cases. Are you starting to get the gist of this chapter, now?

Bring the dial to Nigel Tufnel's proverbial "11," and you'll see folks hunting deer-sized game with the big sticks: 7mm STW and 7mm Remington Ultra Magnum, .300 Weatherby Magnum, .300 Remington Ultra Magnum, and the beastly .30-378 Weatherby Magnum. These are some huge cases, ones with capacities that sometimes exceed 100 grains of powder. Their velocities are way up there. If these tickle your fancy, so be it, I won't judge, but be sure and use only the best of bullets, so you have something to eat after you pull the trigger! Ol'

Grumpy Pants picked up a .300 RUM for long-range caribou on Quebec's tundra, and it works fine. He and I often butt heads about whether I can make the same long-range shot he can with that big case, if I'm shooting my .300 Winchester. He insists the 180-grain bullet leaving the muzzle at 3,350 fps allows him to all but eliminate hold-over out to 300 yards, while I maintain that my 180-grain bullet flying at a muzzle velocity of 2,950 fps is enough for me to hit the target with a six-inch holdover at the same distance. I know my rifle as well as he knows his, and I'd like to think I can shoot as well as he can. His rifle kicks a hell of a lot harder and seems to waste more meat, but him being my dad, I often shake my head and walk away muttering.

Some guys love the bigger bores (yup, count me among them), and like

(Photo courtesy Massaro Media Group & J.D. Fielding Photography)

The .45-70 Government with a 305-grain hollowpoint makes a great deer and black bear load for the thick woods, where shots are at close range.

to use them on deer-sized game, simply because they are such fans of the rifles. If this is you, the 8mm Magnum and .338 bore fans, you can effectively use your favorite rifles on deer-sized game by choosing the lightest bullets available. The 180-grain bullets of any manufacture are available for the 8mm bore, and there is a decent selection of .338-inch diameter bullets suitable for deer hunting; the Barnes TSX in 160- and 185-grain and the Nosler Ballistic Tip 180-grain bullet come quickly to mind. In the .358-inch caliber, Hornady, among others, makes a great 200-grain bullet that can be served up at deer-worthy velocities without damaging too much meat, and even the venerable .375-inch bore has a 235-grain listing that provides a great opportunity for taking your big gun out into the deer woods. I like a Barnes TSX 235-grain in my .375 H&H Magnum for deer and bear in my native Adirondacks. Many .45-70s see duty in the deer woods, too, and although limited in range by the round's rainbow-like trajectory, this old classic has accounted for more than its fair share of game. A 305-grain hollowpoint has performed just fine in Dad's Browning Model 1886. Again, choosing a bullet to suit the task at hand is part of the fun of being a handloader!

Handgun hunters who choose to pursue deer-sized game should probably look to cartridges in the .357 Magnum class as a minimum, using heavy-for-caliber bullets of good construction, to be sure the vitals are reached. The .41 Magnum, 10mm Auto, .44 Magnum, .45 ACP, and .45 (Long) Colt are better choices, as they throw heavier projectiles. Being proficient with your weapon and having great confidence in your ammunition is a must for any hunter, but particularly so for the handgun hunter. Hours spent shooting at the bench at different ranges with your handloaded ammunition will help you guarantee success.

Let's move up the ladder to the next size of big game, to the brown bear, elk, moose, and the large African antelope species, such as wildebeest, kudu, and eland. Game of this size is what originally started the great Elmer Keith versus Jack O'Connor celebrity death match, back in the day, the big-slow-bullet-for-penetration versus the speedy-light-bullet-for-hydraulic-shock argument. Where does this argument stand now?

If, today, we had access only to the bullets available in the 1940s and '50s, I would have to have taken the side of Elmer Keith and big/slow. Of the standard cup-and-core bullet, Keith praised its virtues as being capable of penetration. I agree with him. O'Connor, on the other hand, believed that a standard bullet from a smaller caliber, when placed in the proper location, would kill just as well. He wasn't totally wrong, because that was a man who could slip a bullet exactly where it needed to go—but many hunters lack the patience to pick the shot the way Jack O'Connor did.

I'll leave the judge's decision to history, but what I do want to say is this: The .270 Winchester about which

The author's .300 Winchester Magnum, loaded with 200-grain Swift A-Frames, worked just fine on safari, in South Africa.

A sampling of available .338-caliber bullets.

(Photos both pages courtesy Massaro Media Group & J.D. Fielding Photography)

O'Connor waxed so poetically has much more muscle now, thanks to advanced bullet technology that simply wasn't available back in O'Connor's time. Whereas the venerable Keith poo-pooed the idea of using .270s and even .30-06s on Elk, today's stout bullets such as the Swift A-Frame, Hornady GMX, Barnes TSX, Nosler Partition and Accubond, and North Fork will make that .270 or ought-six into a perfectly viable rifle for all the above mentioned species.

I was shocked, while researching my first safari, one in pursuit of gemsbok, kudu, eland, etc., to find my guide recommended bringing my favorite deer rifle, a .300 Winchester Magnum. Surely I thought I would need a much bigger rifle for the pursuit of the larger African plains game species! Nope. Modern bullets had already proven to my PH that the .300 had adequate killing power, and my familiarity with the rifle would ensure I could place the bullet precisely

where instructed. For that adventure with my .300, I chose the 200-grain Swift A-Frame (to hedge my bets against the largest of antelope, the eland), and had a great time with it. This combination would also very effectively take moose and elk here in North America.

The .338 Winchester Magnum has long been a favorite for elk hunters, and that makes sense. The larger-diameter bullets, those weighing between 200 and 250 grains, have a more dramatic effect on the large cervids and antelope. The .338s and .35-caliber rifles also make a great choice for black bear. Yes, I'm fully aware that many bears are taken with common deer calibers, but, if you've ever had to look for a wounded bear in the willow thickets of Quebec, you might understand why I prefer a heavier projectile. Bears have teeth and claws, after all! The .338s and .35s can be loaded with 200-grain bullets for lighter game, then revved

Flat-point and cup-point North Fork solids in the .375-inch caliber, both weighing 300 grains. Both are suitable for the largest African game animals.

(Photos both pages courtesy Massaro Media Group & J.D. Fielding Photography)

up with a 250-grain bullet for moose and eland. If you don't plan on leaving the North American continent on your hunting adventures, a .338- or .35-bore rifle can make a great companion to your favorite deer rifle to round out your arsenal.

The biggest mammals on Earth require a large-bore rifle with adequate killing power. In this group of animals I shall include bison, brown bear, hippopotamus, Cape buffalo, and elephant—the dangerous game. Here in North America, we normally don't have a legally established caliber minimum, but they certainly do in Africa.

The sheer size of bison and the ferocity of a brown bear should indicate that something large is required, and I think that the .338-inch diameter cartridges are a sensible minimum. They can launch a high sectional density, 250-grain bullet at velocities from 2,400 fps to 2,800 fps, gener-

ating a sensible amount of kinetic energy to handle these huge animals. The various .35 calibers, like the .35 Whelen, .350 Remington Magnum, and the .358 Norma Magnum, are also well suited, as is the venerable .375 Holland & Holland Magnum. No one wants to face a wounded grizzly bear in an alder thicket, so be sure and use something befitting these great bruins. For these powerful cartridges, the Nosler Partition, Swift A-Frame, Barnes TSX, Woodleigh Weldcore, and Speer Grand Slam are all great choices for the biggest of North American animals.

The dangerous game of Africa present a unique conundrum. Most African countries require a minimum bore diameter of .375-inch for hunting the Big Five or Dangerous Seven, and I think this is a sensible minimum. The 9.3mm (.366-inch diameter) cartridges are allowed in some places, Zimbabwe comes to mind, but, generally speaking, I believe the power of the .375 H&H Magnum or .375 Ruger is what is needed to cleanly take these very large creatures. Certainly, leopard and even lion can effectively be taken with lesser calibers, and that is legal in some countries. But, the Cape buffalo and, especially, elephant, require a large bore and a good bullet. There are many big-bores to choose from for game like this. The most popular, far and away, is the aforementioned .375 Holland & Holland Magnum. It is a flexible cartridge with a wide range of bullets ranging from 210 grains up to and including some African-made 380-grain bullets. The classic combination uses a 300-grain bullet driven to about 2,500 feet per second. Using a medium- to slow-burning powder, that velocity can be easily reached. I like to load my .375 H&H with IMR4064, IMR4350, or Reloder 15. Many powders in this realm can produce both excellent velocity and accuracy.

Buffalo can live up to their reputation as "Black Death." To take them cleanly and quickly demands a premium bullet. The same bullets I mentioned for brown bear and bison will perform well on Cape buffalo. For the African elephant, using a .375 solid (a bullet constructed of a homogenous metal, or appearing as a steel-covered lead bullet), is most definitely required. The skull of an elephant has more than two feet of honeycombed bone that must be penetrated to reach the brain. A Barnes Banded Solid, Hornady DGS, North Fork Solid, or Woodleigh Solid should do the trick.

The .416 Remington Magnum is a good choice of cartridge for the biggest game. It is shown here with 400-grain Swift A-Frame bonded-core bullets.

The .458 Winchester Magnum and the huge .500 Nitro Express, two cartridges designed for stopping power!

There are several cartridges that step up the velocity in the .375-inch diameter, such as the .375 Weatherby, .378 Weatherby, and .375 Remington Ultra Magnum. As with any case that increases the velocity, a premium bullet will always perform better, due to the higher velocities that accompany impact. The real beauty of the .375s is their flexibility, especially when you handload for them. They have manageable recoil, while producing over 4,000 ft-lbs of muzzle energy. They can be flat-shooting with 250- and 270-grain bullets for plains game and, yet, with a proper 300-grainer, can effectively be used on buffalo and elephant.

The next step up from the .375 bores are the .40-calibers. The .404 Jeffery (.423-inch), the .450/400 (.411-inch) and the .416 Rigby and .416 Remington Magnum (.416-inch) are all reputable dangerous-game guns. They offer a heavier bullet of larger diameter and are more effective on the big guys, yet you might say you start to lose the flexibility of the .375s. It is in this class of cartridge that you really start to see the financial benefits of loading your own, as factory ammunition can get very expensive.

I like the .416s, as they have a good selection of bullets. I believe they are just about ideal for buffalo. My own sweetheart is a Winchester Model 70 in .416 Remington, affectionately named "Cocoa," for its dark stained stock. I've spent a lot of time at the bench with this rifle; with the 1.5-5x20mm scope, I can consistently print one-inch three-shot groups with it, pushing the 400-grain bullets to an even 2,400 fps on the chronograph.

This equates to 5,000 ft-lbs of energy at the muzzle, a recipe for success, when pitted against any large thing with four feet and a heartbeat. I've used this combination on buffalo with great success and anticipate an elephant hunt using 400-grain Barnes Banded Solids. The venerable .416 Rigby produces the same ballistics, but at the cost of burning over 100 grains of powder in that big case. It is an undeniable classic, but I will say it has more recoil than the comparable Remington design.

The .45-caliber safari rifles are even more specialized, and they are usually reserved for the biggest species. They can launch a 500-grain bullet at velocities of 2,100 to 2,600 fps. The .458 Winchester Magnum is among the most popular in this caliber range, capable of being loaded in a long-action (.30-06 length), and of pushing the 500-grain bullets to 2,100 fps.

There is one drawback to the .458 Winchester, its case capacity. The case is based on the .375 H&H, cut down and blown out to be nearly straight-walled. With this design, the handloader is almost always forced to use compressed loads of powder to achieve acceptable velocities; a compressed load is one in which there is no room for the powder to move in the case, as the bullet physically compresses it during the bullet seating process. Many stick powders take up too much room in the case to get the 500-grainers to that 2,100 fps mark. One powder that worked out very well for me was Hodgdon's H335. It is a ball powder that gave uniform velocities and good accuracy.

Jack Lott enhanced the .458 Winchester design by elongating the case to the full H&H length of 2.850 inches, making the job of handloading much easier. The .458 Lott has some cool features. For one, it's much easier to load for, having a larger case capacity than the .458 Winchester. Because of this, you can obtain higher velocities than with the .458 Winchester. Finally, in a pinch, you can shoot .458 Winchester ammunition in the Lott chamber without issue. Hornady makes good .458 Lott cases.

As you might imagine, when you start pushing those huge 500-grain bullets, the recoil ramps up tremendously. My advice is this: sight in your rifle and develop your load on the shooting bench and then get off it! These big guys are much more comfortable to shoot offhand or off shooting sticks than they are to shoot from the bench. Also, buy the best quality scope you can afford, because a .458 will chew up cheap optics faster than you can buy them!

What al this boils down to, if you're looking for a battery of rifles to cover the entire world and load for them, pick a sensible, medium caliber between .270 and .308 diameter and couple it with a big-bore of .375 through .458. With the selection of bullets and powders available today, you then have a common-sense, complementary pair of rifles suitable for hunting anywhere in the world. These days, my own one-two punch consists of a .300 Winchester Magnum and my .416 Remington Magnum. I sometimes use different rifles when hunting around my home, but, when traveling to hunt abroad, I grab this combination more often than not.

LOADING FOR LONG-RANGE

There's a trend in hunting and shooting these days, one I've been seeing for a number of years. This trend highlights and encourages shooting at very, very long ranges.

Competitive shooting is a wonderful sport, and the greatest risk to participating in it is that your feelings are hurt when you don't shoot as well as you wanted to. In the hunting world, though, it is a much different game. Long-range shots at unwounded game can be, simply put, unethical. I've seen television shows and magazine articles that claim one-shot kills at 700-plus yards. I'm not saying this can't be done, but I have a hard time with the casual attitude. One does not simply

buy a super-magnum 20x scope, take a glance at a drop chart, and proclaim themselves a shooter capable of killing at these distances. Your chosen setup must deliver enough energy upon impact to ensure a humane kill. It's not nearly as easy as some make it out to be.

The hunting debate aside, let's discuss some loading techniques for hitting distant targets.

First, you must have an understanding of the cartridge you're shooting. What is the cartridge's safe velocity potential? Higher velocity results in a flatter trajectory, and that lessens the holdover (the amount of elevation above the target needed to allow for the gravitational effect on the bullet). Which bullet should you choose to resist wind drift and retain energy? How do you get precise accuracy?

(Photos both pages courtesy Massaro Media Group & J.D. Fielding Photography)

Best-quality rifles and optics are required for true long-range shooting. The Leupold scope shown on this .338 Lapua is one of the best available and will hold up to the terrific recoil of the round without losing its zero.

Large-diameter "bull" barrels are often employed on long-range target rifles.

I'm going to start with the last question first. Accuracy is measured in "minutes of angle." There are 60 minutes in one degree, so a minute of angle is an arc of $\frac{1}{60}$-degree. When a rifle is said to be capable of shooting minute-of-angle groups, it is understood that the extreme spread (center to center) of a three- or five-shot group will be no more than the sine of one minute of angle at the distance to the target. At 100 yards, the equation works like this:

The measure of one minute is expressed as a decimal portion of a degree (divide 1 by 60) and the sine of that number is taken. You then multiply that number by 300 feet (100 yards) and then again by 12 to convert feet to inches. If my abacus is correct, one minute of angle (MOA) at 100 yards is equal to an extreme group spread of 1.047 inches.

Now, this minute of angle is a projecting cone, one that gets wider as the distance gets further. Thus, MOA at 200 yards is 2.094 inches, at 300 yards it's 3.142 inches, and so on. Most rifles considered good for long-range use will shoot three-shot groups under 1 MOA and, preferably, ½-MOA.

What we want to do, when we know we'll be shooting at distance, is create ammunition that will keep that group spread to a minimum, obviously so that we can more efficiently and reliably place the bullet on the target. To do this, every step in the loading of your ammunition must be done much more precisely than the ammunition you would produce for shorter ranges, as any error or deviation will be magnified at those greater distances. Let's get down to the nitty-gritty.

Cases should be trimmed to a uniform length and checked with a micrometer. I like to use the cases of the same headstamp and often the same lot, so that the case capacity is as uniform as possible; different brands of cases can be made to different thicknesses, so the volume of the case (inside dimension) can vary. By using the same brand or lot of cases, you can remove as much of that variation as possible.

When installing primers, some precision shooters prefer a handheld priming tool, so that they can feel the primers being seated to a uniform depth. For certain, every individual powder charge *must* be weighed and tolerances held strictly. When seeking this level of accuracy, I also weigh the bullets I have chosen and separate them into groups, using only bullets that have the same weight within a limit of 0.1- or 0.2-grain.

Bullet seating depth uniformity is *critical*. Once the load data has been established at the shooting bench, all future ammunition should be loaded to these specifications, to reproduce the accuracy. Seating depth variations can change the accuracy, so I use a micrometer to verify that my seating die hasn't come out of adjustment and seated my bullets either too deep or out too far. There are several companies that make "precision" or "competition" dies, on which the seating plug has a dial-adjustable mechanism to allow for better control of seating depth. For ultra-precise ammunition, I feel these are a worthwhile investment. Redding Competition Seating Dies are one of my favorites.

Now that you've adhered to the stringent loading of your ammunition, you must examine the rifle to eliminate other factors that may hinder you from hitting your target. While this is not a book on rifles, it must be stated that the best ammunition cannot function well through a rifle that is not well tuned.

Examine the rifle's trigger and make sure it has a clean, crisp pull, not too heavy, not too light, with little creep or over-travel. A gunsmith can tune or replace your trigger if need be. Make sure the action is properly bedded and that the barrel isn't hitting the stock in a way that will affect accuracy. Be certain the scope bases and rings are installed correctly and tightly enough so as not to come loose, and that the rifle scope is mounted so that the vertical crosshair is perfectly aligned with the centerline of the bore—in no way should the reticle be canted. If perfectly aligned, the bullets will drop on a plumb line, when holding over the bull's-eye. If not, at long distances, your shots will drop either to the left or to the right, depending on how the reticle is canted.

Choosing the proper bullet for long-range shooting is mandatory. You'll want something with a high ballistic coefficient, so as to retain as much velocity and energy downrange as possible. A boat-tail bullet often gets the nod. Round-nosed and semi-spitzer bullets have too much drag, and their velocities (and therefore energies) drop off much faster than the boat-tail spitzer design. Most long-range shooters tend to choose a heavier bullet weight, even though they cannot be loaded to be fired as fast as a lighter bullet of the same caliber. The heavy bullet invariably bucks the wind better, and wind drift at long ranges can pose quite a problem, especially when the wind varies along the bullet's path (which it will).

Doping the wind is almost an art form. If I'm in a situation where the possibility of a true long-range shot exists, I usually choose a bullet that will best resist wind drift and increase my chances of shooting where I'm aiming. Many of the polymer-tipped boat-tail bullets I've previously described will fit this bill, as will the lineup of hollowpoint boat-tail bullets suitable for hunting. If you need something for very long-range hunting (and by this I mean more than 400 yards), take a long look at the energy the bullet will have at the longer ranges. A good loading manual will give this information. There are oodles of sources for accepted minimum energy for adequate killing power on different size game animals. I personally like to adhere to this general idea, as best as possible.

LOAD DEVELOPMENT

As you ponder the possibilities of building the perfect load for your rifle and shooting situation, you must be sure that the chosen combination will provide the accuracy and velocity you desire. This process is known as "load development," and it's really what this chapter has been leading up to. I'll use the popular .30-06 Springfield as a hypothetical example.

Let's suppose my goal is to develop a good load for deer-sized game. I don't need a super-tough bullet, yet you want good expansion and penetration. After settling on the Sierra 150-grain spitzer,

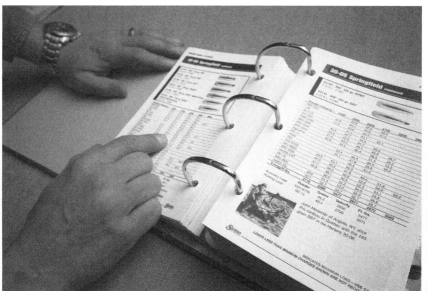

(Photo courtesy Massaro Media Group & J.D. Fielding Photography)

Reloading manuals provide a great wealth of information about the possible bullet and powder combinations for each cartridge. Shown here is the Sierra Edition V manual.

a standard cup-and-core bullet with a good reputation for deer-sized game, I resize and trim up a bunch of once-fired Federal '06 brass.

Sierra's *Rifle & Handgun Reloading Manual, Edition V* indicates that the data was developed using a Federal 210 Large Rifle primer, so I pick up a couple hundred of those primers to start with. Now I must choose a powder. The Sierra Manual offers more than 20 to choose from. Also offered in this manual are recommendations for an "Accuracy Load" and a "Hunting Load."

The first uses a load of 59.6 grains of Hodgdon's H4831 SC, giving 2,800 fps, and the latter uses 53.4 grains of Ramshot BigGame powder for 2,900 fps. If you like either of these, so be it, but both the loads are on the high side of the listed charge weights for these powders, so you must start with a lighter weight to be sure there are no pressure issues with your particular rifle. Because of that, I'm going to choose a more universal powder for my hypothetical loading: IMR4064. It's a middle-of-the-road powder, useful in a wide variety of other cartridges, and (usually) readily available. With this powder, the manual gives us a charge range of a minimum of 44.9 grains (2,600 fps) to a maximum of 52.1 grains (3,000 fps). (Remember that, just as you should never load past the maximum recommended charge, you should also never load below the listed minimum. Under-loading a case is actually quite possibly more dangerous than overloading one!)

The bullets will be seated to Sierra Manual's test COL of 3.225 inches. Since I'm looking for distance work and because there's such a wide range of charge weights I can use, I'd recommend a starting load of an even 45.0 grains and load six rounds for two three-shot groups. I'd then place them in a plastic bag and label the bag with the load data. From there, I load in batches of either three or six rounds, increasing the powder charge for each batch by one grain, until I've reach a load of 52.0 grains (just under the maximum). Each load batch will be placed in its plastic bag and clearly labeled with its load.

Now it's time to hop in the ol' family truckster and head to the shooting range. Rifle, ammunition, targets, hearing and eye protection, cleaning rod and patches, sandbags or some other rifle rest, and a notebook are gathered together for this venture. I like the rifle to be thoroughly clean at this time, but I toss some fouling ammunition—rounds that won't be included in the accuracy test, but will warm the barrel a bit and deposit some minimal residue—in the bag, too. Fouling rounds can be some leftover factory rounds or other odds and ends. Doesn't matter, just keep them separate from your for-group rounds. At the shooting bench, I shoot one fouling round to blow any oil out of the bore and foul the bore. Now I can start to assess the accuracy potential of the loads we've made.

I fire a three-shot group of the lowest powder charge load and assess the group size. It doesn't matter where on the target the load hits, as I'll ultimately adjust the scope for my pet loads, but you would like to see a group.

I'll repeat this for each batch, allowing the barrel to cool between groups, so that barrel heat doesn't open up my groups wider than they should be, and recording the group results against the load data. I make certain that the rifle is well rested into sandbags or whatever other rifle rest I've a mind to use. Also I make sure the fore-end of the stock isn't clamped down into anything, so that the barrel can move freely during the shot. This is where my (and yours!) shooting technique requires the utmost attention—take your time! Finally, every 10 to 15 shots, run a dry patch down the bore to avoid a dirty bore, but I don't want it squeaky clean.

When I'm running load development tests like this, I keep a series of notes in my notebook, recording the group size of each different load, and I watch for pressure signs such as sticky extraction or cratered primers along the way. If I find pressure signs, I will not shoot any of the loads with a heavier charge weight, because I have found my rifle's maximum pressure for that bullet/case/powder combination. What I'm after, with this rather rigorous testing, is accuracy. The charge weight that gives the tightest group is the one I look at, much more than I do the velocity it gives. My personal theory is this: It is more important that the bullet be delivered where it needs to be, than whether I've squeezed the last 100 fps out of the case. If the smallest of the groups still don't meet my accuracy requirements or expectations, I will load more rounds, varying the powder charge by 0.2-grain above and below the tightest group weight

(and so long as I don't exceed the manual's listed maximum load or go above the charge weight that gave me high pressure signs). Repeat the three-shot test data and, with any luck, I'll have found the accuracy I like. If not, it's time to repeat the test process with a new powder and/or primer brand.

When I finally settle on the load that gives me the accuracy I'm after, I then break out the chronograph and shoot 10 shots of that particular load, to establish a good average velocity. I try to observe the velocity as close to the temperature at which I'll be hunting or shooting, to minimize the effects that temperature has on powder. If the velocity is not where I want it, I may have to try a different powder that will give higher

CASE STUDY

▶ When loading for a particular cartridge, it truly pays to do as much research on that case as you can. Some cases have a powder that suits it very well. For example, the .22-250 Remington and Hodgdon H380, the .308 Winchester and IMR4064, and the .270 Winchester and H4831 are known, proven entities. That is not to say that other powders won't work well, but these combinations have stood the test of time and, more often than not, provide a good starting point. The reloading manuals in print toady tell a tale born from thousands of hours of testing and should be respected for that.

velocities at acceptable pressures, while still delivering the accuracy I need. I carefully record the case brand/powder type/charge weight/primer/bullet combination for that rifle in my loading notes and can then reproduce the accuracy I've worked so hard to obtain.

Once the group size and velocity have been established and are acceptable, I look up the trajectory of the specific bullet in question at the velocity given by the chronograph. I usually make a drop chart on the back of a business card, telling me how much holdover is required for shots beyond the distance that rifle is zeroed. Let's say this particular Sierra 150-grain bullet I loaded is moving at 2,850 fps at the muzzle, according to the chronograph. The Ballistic Coefficient of this bullet is right around 0.340 and, when I consult a trajectory chart, I'll find that the rifle is likely best zeroed for 200 yards; this means the arc of the bullet will rise and then lower to strike the bull's-eye of the target at 200 yards. The same chart will indicate that, with such a zero, I must sight the scope to have the bullet strike the target 1.9 inches high at 100 yards, hold eight inches above my point of aim to hit a target at 300 yards, and 24 inches high at 400 yards. This trajectory curve also tells me that, if I align the scope as described, a shot at 100 yards will strike no more than two inches high, yet a 225-yard shot will only be two inches low. Most hunting shots are taken at ranges under 225 yards, and a laser rangefinder will aid in making those long-range shots.

The same process must be repeated for each type and weight of bullet you choose to use. It is not uncommon to have four or five different loads for a particular rifle, especially a rifle that is asked to perform many different tasks. That .30-'06 we've been talking about may be loaded with 125-grain bullets for coyotes and other varmints, or loaded with 220-grain bullets for bears and other large beasts A simple adjustment of the rifle scope is all that's needed for each load, once properly developed.

This is only one example of load development. There are many bullet weights to choose from and experiment with for the .30-06, just as there are for the myriad other cartridges we have today. This kind of load development, then, is a good part of why you've chosen to handload in the first place. Another reason is that each rifle or pistol will have minute differences in their construction and slight variations in the barrels. Some are "tight" or smaller than specified bore diameter. Others are "loose," larger than specified bore diameter. The tight barrels often produce higher velocities, but reach maximum pressures sooner than the loose ones. When handloading, it is important to build each load specific to the firearm you intend to shoot it through, to avoid damaging the gun or, worse, hurting yourself or others. Common sense should always prevail and safety should always come first. Observing the rules will keep your guns happily fed for a lifetime.

The load development process must be repeated for each type and weight of bullet you choose to use. It is not uncommon to have four or five different loads for a particular rifle, especially a rifle that is asked to perform many different tasks.

(Photo courtesy Massaro Media Group & J.D. Fielding Photography)

These are 10mm Auto cartridges, with 155-grain Speer Gold Dot bullets. These fed very well through a Dan Wesson 1911-type pistol.

Load development for your pistol or revolver, unless you're a competitive shooter of the NRA-regulated bull's-eye crowd, generally doesn't revolve around hair-splitting accuracy as much as it does creating rounds for consistent, reliable functioning. Just as it is with rifle load development, you must look at the job you intend your handgun handloads to perform. If you want a .38 Special wadcutter for punching paper, the approach will be different than it is if you're cooking up some heavy loads for deer hunting. Another example would be loads for the many pistol shooters who participate in time-based competitions. These folks want a lighter load that will allow them to get on target quickly after the gun recoils, and they also need reliable feeding. Jams cost precious seconds. The balance for such a shooter is one between accuracy (enough of it) and reliability.

Once you choose the bullet for your pistol, your load development proceeds much the same way it was outlined in the .30-06 example above, except that I would load two-dozen rounds or so for each powder charge batch. Once I had assured myself that the pressures were safe and the accuracy acceptable, I would then shoot two or three magazines of the favored load, to ensure I have reliable feeding. Most pistol shooters know that many semi-autos seem to have an objection to certain bullet profiles. My pal Bill Loëb, for instance, has a Dan Wesson 10mm semi-auto that loves the 155-grain Speer Gold Dot loads I made for him, yet has an aversion to feeding the 180-grain lead truncated cone profile. More than likely, the feed ramp just doesn't agree with the bullet design, but you won't know this until you work up your loads and do the work.

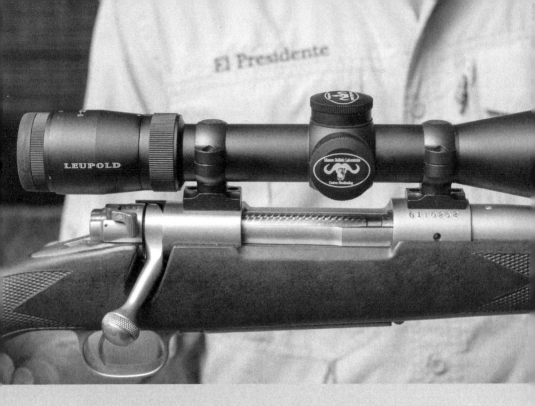

LOADING VERSATILITY EXEMPLIFIED

The custom engraved Leupold VX6 2-12x40 rifle scope on the author's .300 Winchester Magnum.
(Photo courtesy Massaro Media Group & J.D. Fielding Photography)

Among big-game hunters, the 7mm and .308-inch bore diameters are universally recognized as being among the most versatile rifle calibers available, with both offering a wide range of bullet weights. The 7mm bore has common weights from 100-grain to 175-grain, while the .308 bore uses 110-grain through 220-grain bullets. I have loaded for many different 7mms, and, while I respect them very much, I have actually spent most of my hunting days behind the trigger of a .30-caliber rifle. With the exception of the bullets heavier than 180 grains, the two calibers are very similar in the fact that they have a selection of bullets suitable for hunting game animals from varmint size through large bears.

One of my favorite rifles is a Winchester Model 70 Classic Stainless chambered in .300 Winchester

Magnum and nicknamed the "Silverback." It has a stainless steel barreled action and a composite stock, making it just about impervious to adverse weather conditions. I bought it used, in 2004, and it just so happened to fit me like a glove.

One of the beautiful features of the .300 Winchester is that it can be loaded to its maximum potential to be a serious long-range rifle, yet can also be loaded down to the same ballistics as the .308 Winchester or .30-06 Springfield for hunting in the northeast woods where the average shot is under 125 yards. I have done exactly that with this rifle. Because of the variety of hunting situations where I carry my .300, I require a versatile rifle scope, one capable of handling very close shooting in the dark conifer woods of the Catskill and Adirondack Mountains in my native New York, yet also suitable for long-range shooting on the wide-open terrain outside of Quebec, on the windy plains of Wyoming, or for plains game in a place like the Kafue Flats, in Zambia. I settled on a Leupold VX6 2-12x42mm with a 30mm main tube. A true 2x on the bottom allows me to shoot at distances as close as 10 yards with no problem picking up the target, yet the top end of 12x is enough magnification for the furthest distances in which I feel confident shooting.

The game animal I hunt most often is whitetail deer. Now, I certainly know you do not need a .300 Winchester to kill a deer, but no one would scoff if you used a .308 Winchester or .30-06 for a deer rifle. Here, in New York, with the exception of some power lines and farm fields, our shots at deer tend to be relatively close, so, again, I require neither a very heavy bullet nor a ton of speed. For this kind of hunting, I chose a 150-grain Sierra flat-based spitzer that gets seated over 68 grains of Reloder 19. This gave me a velocity of 2,850 fps, which is right on par with the .30-06, and even a .270 Winchester pushing a 150-grain bullet. This handload works perfect for deer, even though it is on the light end of the round's loading data.

I've taken my .300 with me on several long-range hunts. The pronghorn antelope is known for its uncanny eyesight and the wide-open treeless prairie it inhabits. Getting close to them is no easy task, and the plains of the American West are notorious for their windy conditions. I wanted a bullet fast enough to produce a relatively flat trajectory, yet heavy enough to buck the wind. I worked up a load using what I feel is the ideal bullet weight for a .300 Magnum, the 180-grain. I tried several and got good results with a Sierra boat-tail and a Hornady flat-base, but the Swift

The .300 Winchester Magnum, with the 180-grain Swift Scirocco II seated over IMR4350.
(Photo courtesy Massaro Media Group & J.D. Fielding Photography)

Scirocco II gave the best results of all in this particular rifle. I actually had two loads that worked out perfect for this bullet, one using Reloder 19 again, and then the one I settled on that used 68.5 grains of IMR4350 in a Remington-Peters case backed by a Federal 215 Large Rifle Magnum primer. This load will print three-shot groups of 0.3-inch, if I do my part on the bench. That work both in loading and bench time ended up being very effective in Wyoming, on a recent pronghorn. I stalked him to within 215 yards, in very windy conditions, and dropped him in his tracks. Could I have made this shot with factory ammo? Sure. But that's not really the point. What makes the difference is that I've worked through the bigger variety of possibilities and load combinations that only reloading can provide, and I *know* what my best loads will do. That's a kind of confidence that doesn't come so easily with factory fodder.

My first African Safari was in 2004, to the Republic of South Africa. As is my usual habit when

I travel, I brought two rifles with me. I had become infatuated with the .375 Holland & Holland Magnum, but I brought a .300 Winchester along in the event of longer shots. Now, one thing about Africa is that you never know what you may see while afield. In pursuit of an impala, you may stumble across the eland of your lifetime, or, while tracking zebra, you may see a wonderful tiny duiker. Point is, you'll need a rifle capable of swiftly taking the biggest animal you intend to hunt. To meet this range of shooting possibilities, I loaded the .300 Winchester with a bullet I feel is well suited to the broad spectrum of African plains game, the 200-grain Swift A-Frame. My rifle is happy with this bullet over 75.0 grains of Reloder 25, in a W-W Super case lit up by the Federal 215M Match Large Rifle Magnum primer. Group sizes average just over one-inch. The chronograph tells a tale of a muzzle velocity at 2,750 fps, so I made a drop chart, zeroed the rifle scope accordingly, and packed my bags. That first safari was wonderful and the .300 did its share of the work, claiming my very first head of African game, a splendid gemsbok bull with 33-inch-long, well-broomed horns. The heavy, stout bullet in the .300 Winchester used on that gemsbok would suffice for any of Africa's antelope, and it's been used by others many times over on game as tough as grizzly bear and lion.

Even with that safari, I wasn't done putting the .300 Winchester through the ringer. I had been studying way too many books on old rifle calibers and the wheels were grinding. I'd read the praises of the .318 Westley Richards, a round using a 250-grain .330-inch diameter bullet at a muzzle velocity of 2,400 fps, and how, at that weight and velocity, the penetration and knockdown power had earned the favor of early twentieth-century hunters. Well, finances being what they were, I couldn't afford to buy a .318 WR, but I *did* have some long, 220-grain, .308-inch round-nosed bullets and a .300 Winchester! If I couldn't buy a .318, maybe I could build the next best thing!

I grabbed my Hornady Interlock 220-grain round-nosed bullets and thumbed through some old reloading manuals looking for a load that would give me 2,400 fps. It wasn't long at all before I saw that 53.0 grains of IMR4064 would yield exactly that, and I proceeded to fill some Remington-Peters nickel-plated cases with that very load. I had some Remington 9½ primers on hand, and that combination worked out very well. Group size hangs around an inch, and the bullet performs very well. I have cleanly taken a black bear and

several deer with it, including an 11-point whitetail that weighed 175 pounds after field dressing. I call this load "I-can't-believe-it's-not-a-Westley."

By now, it should be plain just how versatile one rifle can be, thanks to handloading. Of course, no one would ever call the .300 Winchester Magnum a small round, so, it's not for everyone. For the shooter who pursues lighter game or wants a target rifle that will be more wind resistant than the .22-caliber centerfires, the .243 Winchester is another example of a versatile caliber for which you should handload. The 6mm bore diameter offers a wider range of bullet weights than the .22-calibers, and it is well suited to performing as both a varmint-class rifle and a good deer/antelope gun. The case is efficient, one based on the .308 Winchester necked down to hold 6mm bullets, and it has the inherent accuracy potential of the .308. It makes an awful lot of sense for the hunter who wants only one rifle for varmint to deer-size range of animals.

On the lighter end of the scale, for woodchucks, prairie dogs, and coyotes, there are a good many varmint bullets available for the .243. Hornady's 58-grain V-Max, Nosler's 55-grain Ballistic Tip, Berger's 69-grain Match Flat Base, and Speer's 70-grain TNT hollowpoint come to mind. These bullets are very frangible, meaning that will expand easily, a design perfect for varmint hunting.

I like two very different powders for the .243 with these bullets, IMR3031 and IMR4350. A suitable load of IMR3031 with the Hornady 58-grain V-Max and a good Large Rifle primer like a CCI200 will yield muzzle velocities in the neighborhood of 3,800 fps. This is performance very close to the .22-250 Remington or .220 Swift, both of which are classic varmint calibers really best suited/limited to that hunting classification. Try and develop your loads so they will give at least MOA accuracy (and, preferably, smaller), and you should be able to consistently hit coyotes and woodchucks out to almost 400 yards with some practice. In fact, I've used a .243 Winchester with lighter bullets to produce some very impressive groups (some ¼-MOA). Hunting varmints out to 300-plus yards (and providing I do my part behind the trigger), the results are always impressive. Several coyotes have gone down "bang-flop."

Many hunters reach for the .243 Winchester when it comes to hunting deer and antelope. I've stated that the 6mm cartridges are on the lower end of the spectrum for this job, as far as I am concerned. However, in the hands of a cool shot, I know for certain that the .243 can be very effective. I recommend using only the 85-, 90-, and 100-grain bullets, and I'd have no problem with a hunter reaching for one of the premium projectiles in this caliber. The Hornady 85-grain Interbond, a 90-grain Swift Scirocco II Nosler AccuBond, or maybe a 100-grain Speer Grand Slam or Nosler Partition should be looked at as viable candidates for deer hunting.

My family friend Col. Le Frogg has a Ruger Model 77 in the matte grey and laminate stock Target/Varmint configuration that loves a 100-grain Nosler Partition over 40.0 grains of Reloder 19, with a CCI200 primer in a Remington case. The Nosler leaves the muzzle at 2,850 fps. This is a very accurate load (and one that makes me believe that Reloder 19 is among the best powders for the .243 Winchester with the heavier bullets). Like most other calibers, if you're looking for retained energy

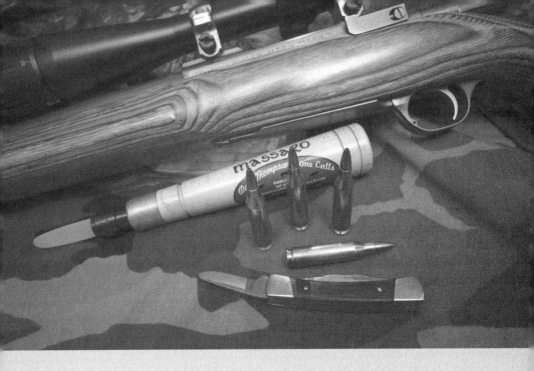

*The .243
Winchester and
hollowpoint bullets
make a very
potent varmint
combination.*
(Photos both pages courtesy
Massaro Media Group & J.D.
Fielding Photography)

at long distances, look to the long, sleek, boat-tail bullets. They will need less holdover when you get out past 250 yards, and they drift less in the wind.

Just in case you're not convinced that reloading can give you the kind of flexibility you would mostly likely struggle to get with factory fodder, and just in case you think this belief is only applicable to "common" cartridges, let's look at the .375 Holland & Holland. This African classic was developed by the prestigious firm of Holland & Holland, in 1912, and was originally loaded with Cordite. It had the privilege of being the first successful belted cases (one that headspaces off the front of the belt, rather than the rim or the shoulder), blending the best features of both rimmed and rimless cases. It gained a respectable reputation immediately.

The big belted case was originally offered with three bullet weights, a 235-grain, a 270-grain, and a 300-grain, but today's bullets are better. I got my first .375 just after the turn of the twenty-first century, a push-feed Winchester Model 70, with the idea of an African safari in mind. I gathered some Federal 215 Large Rifle Magnum primers, Winchester cases, and the Grumpy Pants-approved IMR4064 powder.

Initial load development didn't go so well with this rifle, but it turns out the rifle had a severe bedding problem. Once I had Hill Country Rifles iron that little wrinkle out, I sat at the bench with my handloads and got good groups with the Speer 235-grain HotCor and Sierra 250-grain boat-tail bullets. Both are good choices for lighter game in both Africa and North America, and I've loaded them for many friends who hunt on both continents. The Sierra 250-grain load I developed worked very well on African plains game. It sat on top of 68.5 grains of IMR4064 that propelled it to 2,750 fps and shot right at MOA accuracy. Dad took a great kudu and gemsbok with my rifle and this load on his first safari. The 235-grain Speer shot very well, also, but is a bit too soft on deer-sized game. The whitetail deer Dad and I have taken with it had a large amount of blood-shot meat and a huge wound channel. I now reserve these bullets for paper. I've recently loaded some of the Barnes TSX 235-grain all-copper bullets for some clients, with great results. Accuracy is as good as you can expect, being under MOA, and the mono-metal bullet will not come apart. Using Reloder 15, a powder the .375 H&H likes very much, and a 235-grain Barnes TSX, you have a pretty flat-shooting, yet low-recoil combination that's well suited for plains game in Africa, or elk, moose, and bear in North America.

Head up the weight scale to the heavier bullets, and you have in your hands a raging beast capable of taking all game on earth. The 270-grain Barnes TSX and Swift A-Frames are great bullets that give good results at lower recoil levels on the largest of mammals, but go on to load the .375 H&H with a premium 300-grain bullet and it will really shine. Many African Profession-

IMR4350 gave excellent results in the .375 H&H case, printing three-shot groups of less than one MOA.

The .375 H&H Magnum, with 300-grain Swift A-Frame bullets.
(Photo courtesy Massaro Media Group & J.D. Fielding Photography)

al Hunters swear that no other cartridge will penetrate as deep as a 300-grain .375-inch bullet. My pet load uses 77.0 grains of IMR4350 under a 300-grain Swift A-Frame, set off by a Federal 215M primer in a Remington case to give me a muzzle velocity of 2,510 fps. This particular load worked wonders for me in South Africa, as well as on a bison hunt in South Dakota.

One of the wonderful properties of the .375 H&H is the ability to put many bullets of different make into the same point of impact. That's important when hunting dangerous game, where a mixture of solids and premium soft-points will be used. My .375 would put 300-grain Swift A-Frames, 300-grain Hornady round-nosed, and 300-grain Hornady Solids all into the same bull's-eye. I once shot a three-shot group, using one each of the three bullets above, into a group that measured 1.1 inches.

CHAPTER 8

WHY DIDN'T THIS WORK OUT?

(Photo courtesy Massaro Media Group & J.D. Fielding Photography)

In this chapter, I'm going to delve into some of the problems and pitfalls that come with loading your own ammunition, from the disappointing to the dangerous. Hopefully, this will allow you to learn from the mistakes of others without having to make them yourself.

If you're like me, you've done your best to adhere to all the rules and guidelines that have been outlined so far. You've read the reloading manuals, learned the history and design of your particular cartridge, tumbled the cases until they are shiny, resized them properly, picked out the bullet, primer, and powder that tickle your fancy, and assembled it all to the best of your ability. As you head to the range, you're as giddy as a five-year-old on Christmas Eve. Then, after settling into the bench, stuffing the shiny little fellas into your sweetheart pistol or rifle, and holding and squeezing, the walk to the target shows disappointing results. The groups are much larger than you've expected. This is the most common problem, and here are some of the causes.

POWDER CHOICE

As I've previously outlined, there are many different types of smokeless powder on the market today, for both pistols and rifles. Some have been around for more than 70 years, while others are just a year or two old.

Rifles, to a greater degree than pistols, are finicky creatures. I've owned and loaded for some that would happily and accurately digest just about any powder I stuffed in the case. Those kinds of guns are a joy. Then, there have been some, like Dad's Ruger Model 77, chambered in .300 Winchester, that seemed to be unhappy with everything I brewed up.

The fact of the matter is, every barrel is different. Accuracy comes from one thing, and that is consistent, repeatable barrel harmonics. The same thing applies to pistols.

There will usually be some suggested powders in the overview of your cartridge choice in the major reloading manuals. Listen to the people who wrote these tomes, as they do research for a living. That said, it may take some experimentation to find *your* recipe, that magic combination of components that provide the level of accuracy you're happy with. Don't be afraid to try a different type or brand of powder (if it's listed in your manual), and certainly don't get married in the first place to a particular powder. There are many websites, social forums, and blogs that discuss the best starting points for a particular cartridge, and the reloading manuals, old and new, provide a great resource for choosing powders. A change in powder has many a time resulted in a rifle shooting sub-MOA groups where before it was minute of softball. By the bye, I found the magic recipe for Dad's .300, using Reloder 25 powder and 200-grain Swift A-Frames. He is, finally, a happy moose hunter.

POWDER CHARGE

The reloading manual will give you a range of powder weights for your cartridge, from the start weight (being the lowest) to the maximum. It is always best and safest to start at the lowest weight and slowly increase the load while watching for pressure signs. Finding the sweet spot is usually a matter of diligent trial and error. Sometimes a small adjustment in the powder charge can result in a dramatic change in group size. My .416 Remington printed 2½-inch groups with my initial loading. This was acceptable, the rifle being intended for the large vitals of the Cape buffalo, but I'm not one to settle. An adjustment of one grain of powder brought the 100-yard group size down to about 0.9-inch. Now, to me, that's pretty impressive for a rifle of that caliber and a 5x scope. The same scenario presented itself in my .308 Winchester and, this time, a 0.2-grain adjustment made all the difference.

When I'm getting close to the accuracy I want via the load development process described in the last chapter, what I usually do is make cartridges in groups of six (for two, three-shot groups), with various powder charges in half-grain increments, then fine-tune the load until I find that which the rifle likes.

BULLET CHOICE

I enjoy using many different bullet makes and models. Some of my rifles prefer long, lean, boat-tailed spitzers,

while others prefer flat-based bullets, either round-nosed or spitzer. I spent a lot of time and money (not to mention stomach lining), chasing my tail and wondering why my .22-250 would not print the 52-grain boat-tail hollowpoint match-grade bullets into the tight little groups I wanted. I tried various powders, different cases, human sacrifice (kidding), all with no luck. My colleague and mentor, Col. Le Frogg, overheard my complaining one day and solved the problem immediately.

"Your barrel's crown is a bit imperfect," he said to me. "Switch to the 53-grain flat-base and call me in the morning."

He was spot on. Switching to the flat-base gave me $^3/_8$-inch three-shot groups, with the same powder charge I'd been using with the 52-grain bullets. Le Frogg had been right, the crown was (and still is) ever so slightly out of round, and the gas-

Sierra's flat-base MatchKing made all the difference in the accuracy of the author's .22-250. You have to experiment.
(Photo courtesy Massaro Media Group & J.D. Fielding Photography)

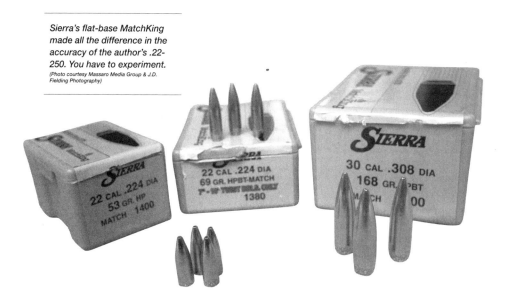

ses were affecting the flight of those boat-tail bullets because of that crown imperfection. I could have had it re-crowned, but it shoots those flat-base bullets so well I haven't bothered. Lesson here: If you're unhappy with your rifle's performance with boat-tails, try a flat-base bullet. The difference in long-range trajectory is minimal at most sane hunting ranges, but the accuracy usually improves dramatically.

The same applies to the pistols. Some barrels prefer the jacketed hollowpoints we love so much, while I've also seen some snub-nosed .38 Specials that will print wadcutters into very tight groups. A finicky 1911 .45 ACP I had would only print 230-grain round-nosed ammunition well; no matter how we loaded 185-grain jacketed bullets, it wasn't happy. Bottom line is, it may take some time to find the particular bullet for your rifle or pistol. Let go of "loving" a particular powder or bullet if it's not working though your gun, because why would anyone want to keep barking up that tree and getting crappy results? That just doesn't make sense. Experiment, switch things up. When you get to the load that sings, you'll be a confident and happy shooter.

MECHANICAL ISSUES

After hunting moose in Quebec, glassing across those long, wide lakes and finally seeing the sheer size of those Kings of Deer, I promptly headed to my local gun shop and purchased a rifle I felt worthy of *Alces Alces*, the .375 Holland & Hol-

Quality bases, rings, and optics help to evaluate accuracy, taking mechanical issues out of the equation.
(Photo courtesy Massaro Media Group & J.D. Fielding Photography)

land Magnum. Proud as a peacock, I bought a set of dies, a couple hundred rounds of brass, and some bullets I really liked the look of. But, no matter what I did, regardless my procedure, I had the same issue: I would put the first shot on paper, the second would hit three inches up and to the right, and the third would land within an inch of the first. Being new to handloading at the time and unwilling to settle for that degree of accuracy, I made a phone call to a custom rifle shop in New Braunfels, Texas, that specializes in fixing these sorts of problems. They told me that my loading wasn't the problem, rather that the barreled action wasn't bedded properly into the stock (an inherent problem with my particular gun model). The rifle was shipped to them and re-bedded and, lo and behold, the problem was solved. That big stick now prints under one-inch groups with 250-, 270-, or 300-grain bullets.

Another rifle I had, a military Mauser conversion, wouldn't group below 2 MOA. Different bullets, powders, and primers were used, all with the same results. The culprit? A military trigger. Creepier than an old man in a van, the trigger broke at about eight pounds. It was virtually impossible to keep the rifle on target while getting this trigger to break. The solution? A premium replacement trigger. I ordered one from Timney, took my time installing it, and ended up reducing the groups to minute of angle or better, depending on the load.

Lesser quality optics and/or bases and rings can also be a source of frustration. Bases that loosen from vibration and rings that don't properly hold the scope or are simply improperly installed can drive you crazy. Purchasing the best bases and rings you can afford is worth every penny you spend. If the hardware won't hold zero, the best handloaded ammunition in the world won't make a bit of difference.

LOADING DIFFICULTY

At the bench, target all set up, hopes higher than Heaven, you load your firearm—except the bolt won't close, the pistol won't chamber a round, the autoloading rifle won't go into battery. Now what?

It's time to reexamine the cases. Did you properly resize them? A bolt-action rifle has the strength to cam-over on a slightly over-sized cartridge, but pumps, levers, and auto-loaders do not. Full-length resizing, described in Chapter 4, is imperative, when it comes to the pump-action, lever-action, and auto-loading rifles (and pistols). The partially sized case can be the bane of the handloader. You must make sure all your resizing dies are properly adjusted, to ensure the ammunition you've worked so hard to make works properly in your firearm. If loading problems do rear their ugly heads, try switching over to small base sizing dies, which will resize the cases all the way to the base.

UNLOADING DIFFICULTY

Okay, it loads fine. You take two deeps breaths, let the last one half-

The primer on the left shows acceptable pressure. It has the same appearance as a new one, with the exception of the firing pin mark. The primer on the right has been flattened and the firing pin mark appears "cratered," showing signs of excessive pressures.

The author's dad, a.k.a. Grumpy Pants (right), explaining the effects of a canted reticle on long-range shooting. He knows what he's talking about!

(Photos courtesy Massaro Media Group & J.D. Fielding Photography)

way out, hold, and gently squeeze … *bang*! But, the action won't cycle. The bolt won't open. You can't extract the cartridge. What does this mean?

You, my friend, have a pressure problem. Pressure is funny thing. It's also a very, very dangerous thing. It can result in a damaged firearm at best, or loss of life at worst. It works like this: Every cartridge is nothing

more than a pressure "chamber." It is made of brass, a malleable metal, and is designed to hold a specific charge of propellant in order to propel the bullet or shot when ignited. If you exceed that pressure limit for which the cartridge was designed, excessive pressure will show its ugly face. In the revolver, it can result in a cracked cylinder. In a rifle, it

A steady, comfortable rest that does not impinge the rifle's fore-end is a must to properly evaluate the accuracy of your handloaded ammunition.
(Photo courtesy Massaro Media Group & J.D. Fielding Photography)

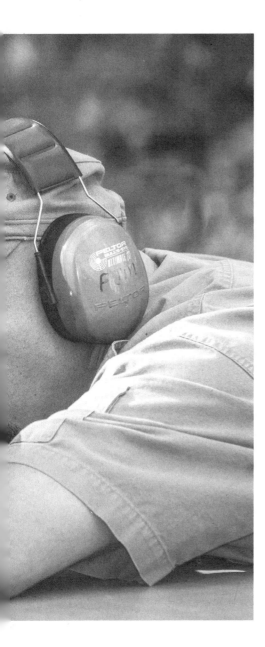

becomes a stuck bolt or, perhaps, a broken extractor. I don't ever want you to experience this, so allow me to identify some symptoms.

If you are able to extract the cartridge but with difficulty, examine the struck primer. If the mark left by the firing pin appears to have a raised crater around the edges or the edges of the primer don't have the nice rounded appearance they did when you seated them, the pressure has become excessive. This means that, *for the particular firearm you are holding*, the load is too hot and it has created excessive and unacceptable pressures.

But, wait, Phil. I loaded these .270 Winchester cartridges in accordance with the manual of the bullet manufacturer. Everything should be fine, no?

In theory, yes, but, there are variables you might not be aware of. First, what is the barrel length of your firearm in comparison to the barrel length of the firearm used in the test data? For every extra inch of barrel, you gain around 25 fps of velocity and the pressure increases accordingly.

An example: The test data shows the loads for the .270 Winchester were fired in a 22-inch barrel, but you've got a 26-inch barrel. This will result in an increase of roughly 100 fps, so the powder charges that proved safe and acceptable in the test rifle have shown excessive pressure in your rifle. Reduce the charges and work up, carefully, until you have a load that is sufficiently accurate and shows no pressure signs.

Another example: My .357 Magnum had its cases stuck in the cylinder one day at the range. I used an appropriate load for the bullet weight, but was still getting pressure problems. I have a six-inch barrel, but the data was tested in a four-inch barrel. Once again, it is imperative to compare your firearm to the test firearm and be aware of any differences.

Many people contact me wondering why their particular rifle or pistol doesn't measure up to the advertised velocities of the ammunition companies or reloading manuals. Often times, the barrel length is again the issue: the advertised velocities were established in a longer (read higher pressure) barrel, and, for you, having a firearm equipped with a shorter barrel, it is only logical that your velocities should be lower. When dealing with Magnum cartridges, they often reach their potential only in long-barreled rifles and pistols, so keep this in mind when you plan a firearm purchase.

Sometimes, groups delivered to the target aren't what we wish for. We blame the load. We blame the trigger. We blame the wind. We blame the fact that Orion isn't aligned with Cassiopeia. It has happened to me, and I'm sure it will happen to you. We just need to be honest enough to admit the ugly truth to ourselves. Say it with me, "I'm not shooting well right now."

When trying to develop and assess a load you've created, you will need to call upon your best shooting skills. The goal is to try and evaluate whether the rifle or pistol delivers consistent results (group size) and, to do that, we have to remove as much of the human error as possible. Shoot-

*A .38 Special
on sandbags.*
(Photo courtesy Massaro
Media Group & J.D.
Fielding Photography)

WHY DIDN'T THIS WORK OUT? **207**

ing from uncomfortable positions or off a shaky rest will not allow you to obtain the true accuracy potential of your handloads, and it will keep you awake at night wondering if the firearm/load combination is the problem or if it was your shooting. Grumpy Pants taught me the basic shooting mechanics at a very young age.

"When you get the rifle settled," he'd tell me, "take two deep breaths, let the last one halfway out, and slowly squeeze the trigger."

I still hear his voice in my head, as if I were 11 again, whether he's with me at the bench or not. You don't want to know when the gun is going to go off, so that you don't tense up and send the shot awry. A slow, smooth trigger pull with "follow-through" (imagine trying to see the bullet rip the paper), will give the best results. Jerking or slapping at the trigger will not give good accuracy.

When developing loads for hard-kicking rifles or pistols, I bring my favorite bolt-action .22 Long Rifle with me. Shooting that rifle in between groups of big-game rifles or pistols helps prevent me from developing a flinch, a tough habit to break once it sets in. With the rimfire rifle, which has virtually no recoil, you can actually see the bullet hit, so it helps me to keep my shooting skills sharp.

I like to shoot from a comfortable bench, built sturdily, and off of sandbags. The sandbag rest allows the rifle to settle down and is, in my opinion, the best

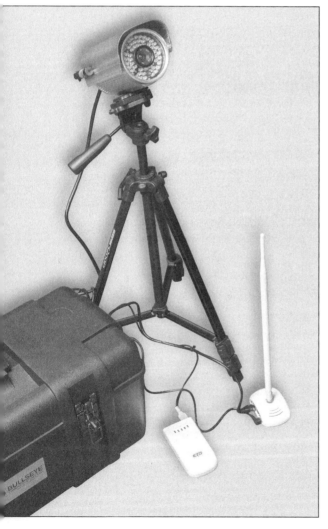

The Bullseye Camera System.
(Photo courtesy Massaro Media Group & J.D. Fielding Photography)

way to eliminate the human element from the equation. Sometimes I use one sandbag under the fore-end of the rifle, other times I'll use one under the fore-end and one under the butt of the stock. When I use only one, I like to hold the rear portion of the stock with my left hand (I shoot right-handed) to help steady the rifle, leaving the fore-end comfortably nestled in the sandbag. The goal is not to impinge the barrel in the fore-end of the stock, thereby allowing it to move freely throughout recoil.

There are vice-type shooting rests available, and they can be a help to hold steady, so long as the fore-end of the rifle is free to move. You never want to put a force on the firearm that won't be there under normal shooting conditions. Doing so will affect the point of impact and group size.

Several shooting friends use a Lead-Sled to absorb the recoil from hard-kicking rifles. I haven't ever used one myself, and I've heard mixed reviews. Some guys swear by them, because the lack of recoil allows them to shoot much better, while other guys tell me about cracked stocks from the way the device holds the firearm. Again, I haven't used them, but if you plan to, please do your research.

When developing pistol loads, I use the same one-sandbag and two-breath technique described for rifle shooting, put I usually place my left hand under my right, for the steadiest hold. This grip works well for me. The goal in either case is to hold the firearm as steady as possible, to give repeatable results.

Hey, speaking of the shooting bench, I found a new company that makes a rather innovative product. Bullseye Camera Systems has a wireless target camera that you set up about 10 feet away from your target, align the laser pointer to the center of the bull's-eye and, when you switch it on, the device interfaces with your Windows-based laptop computer, iPhone, or iPad. In other words, the target images are delivered to the device you choose, at the bench, and the 100-yard shuffle is a thing of the past! You can isolate individual shots or groups of shots on your device, record group size, etc., out to 600 yards with the basic model and out to 2,000 yards with the extended range version. Now, not only is it really cool to have the group size and image recorded on your phone or laptop, but think about how much time you'll save waiting for your heart rate to slow down after you've walked 100 yards (or more) to the target and then again for the return trip. It *really* pays off at the 300-yard plus ranges. This is a truly ingenious product. I am a bit spoiled, having a personal 200-yard rifle range on premises, but I can imagine that these camera systems will be a hit with just about any rifle or pistol club in America!

Now, let's examine some problems as they occur at the reloading bench.

There's nothing worse than a stuck case. You seat the case in the shellholder, work the press handle, and *bam*! You simply can *not* remove that dirty bugger from the sizing die. Maybe you've even ripped off the

FRUSTRATED?!

Follow these simple steps to remove a stuck case

1. Case rim ripped away, you stare at a case stuck in the resizing die.

2. A specific-size hole must be drilled through the case web.

3. That hole must be tapped with the supplied tapping tool.

4. The hardened screw is threaded into the tapped hole in the web.

case rim trying. Ten seconds ago you had a great new hobby, now you're reaching for the rocks glass and two fingers of bourbon. You're asking yourself, *Why me, Lord, why me?*

Well, friend, we've all done it. In fact, this happens so often that many companies have marketed the solution: *the stuck case remover.* I use an RCBS model. With it I take the provided drill bit to drill through the flash hole and into the case's web, and then I use the provided tap to thread the newly drilled hole. The kit includes a hardened screw that threads into the tapped hole and, one crank at a time, it draws the stuck case out of the resizing die.

Why did it happen? An insufficient amount of case lube. Lubricating the cases in just the proper fashion is important. Not enough lubrication and the cases will stick in the die like peanut butter to the roof of your mouth. Too much lubricant, and the cases develop those funky little shoulder dents that can ruin the appearance of your shiny, wonderful little creations.

Cartridge cases, as I've said, are generally made of brass or nickel-coated brass. Brass is used primarily because of its malleability, or ability to mold, bend, and flow. It is much less rigid than steel, and the cases can be reused several times. However, they don't last forever. It is important to keep a record of how many times the cases have been fired, resized, and reloaded. When brass cartridge cases have reached the end

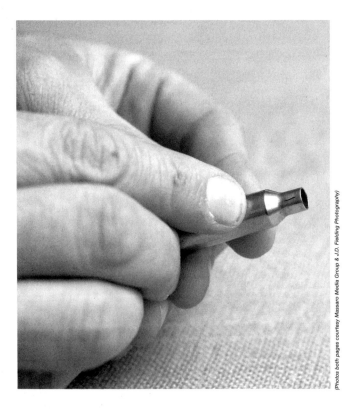

(Photos both pages courtesy Massaro Media Group & J.D. Fielding Photography)

The neck of this .22-250 Remington has split from being fired and resized too many times. Toss it away!

of their days, they lose their malleability and become brittle. When this happens, they are prone to split in the neck. When you see this symptom, it is crucial that you remove and destroy these cases. *They are not safe.* As expensive as cartridge cases are these days, there is no reason to use unsafe components.

Sometimes, after running the case through a seating die set up to give a roll crimp (e.g., the .45 Long Colt, .357 Magnum, .45-70 Government, and many hard-recoiling safari calibers), you may see that the case appears crumpled or that the shoulder area is bulged or rolled. The problem? The seating die is adjusted too low, giving too much crimp and actually crushing the case as it does so. You don't ever want to try and fire ammunition that is bulged or has a rolled shoulder, as it can be dangerous to the weapon and the shooter.

Obviously, if you have this problem, you need to adjust your seating die. But why not cut to the chase and

The .458 Winchester Magnum on the right is a victim of too much crimp and not enough flare. That caused the case to crumple.

prevent the problem in the first place? When I'm starting a new load, I often use three or four dummy rounds (bullet and case, no primer or powder) to adjust the dies properly.

CHAPTER 9

SPECIALTY SITUATIONS

L et's get into some of the different situations that are noteworthy and discuss the ins and outs of dealing with them, though in no particular order.

MILITARY RIFLES
AND MILITARY BRASS

Military brass can be of great value to the reloader. The surplus, once-fired brass can often be had at a small fraction of the cost of purchasing new brass. But those shooters who shoot military ammunition or use military brass for their rifles need to pay special attention to the techniques necessary to prepare these particular cases for reloading.

There are a couple things you need to keep in mind about military brass. First, the case walls are generally thicker than in the sporting version of the same case. Second, the primers are crimped and often sealed into the primer pocket.

Let's handle the second problem first. A tedious inspection of all military cases is in order, as sometimes these cases are not manufactured to the same tight tolerances as you'll usually find in their sporting counterparts. I tumble my military brass first, before resizing, so I can better inspect the cases for split necks, severe dents, or rims that are bent from heavy extraction. After that's done, I move to the primer.

Most military brass has a crimp to hold the primer in. The case on the left has the crimp ring, the case on the right does not.
(Photos both pages courtesy Massaro Media Group & J.D. Fielding Photography)

On military brass, there is a small band of brass at the rim of the primer pocket, designed to hold the primer in place during the most rigorous battle conditions and rough handling of military ammunition. This poses a pair of problems to the reloader. One, it is more difficult to remove the spent primer. Two, the crimp ring must be removed before installing a new primer.

I recommend installing a hardened decapping pin to help remove those wedged-in military primers. You'll feel the difference in the first few rounds of military brass you try to resize; there is a considerable amount of extra resistance when you try and pop out that primer. The hardened pin will not bend or break as easily as a standard pin, so it lets you get a bit more "gorilla" when removing the primer.

Once that primer is removed, you have to get rid of that little crimp ring that's built into the primer pocket.

There are two methods used to make this little obstruction go away: either cut it out or swage it out.

There are many hand tools that will cut or ream out the military crimp. Some are very simple, like the Hornady or Lyman pocket reamer, while others work on a hand crank principle, such as the L.E. Wilson reamer that works in conjunction with the company's case trimming device. Some cutting tools used to remove the military crimp are built for use with electric case preparation machines. The RCBS case-prep station, for instance, has an attachment specially designed for removing the military crimp from both large and small primer pockets. It uses the rotating heads on the top of the machine and easily cuts out the crimp at the higher rpm settings. Hornady offers a similar tool for its case trimming machine.

The second method, swaging, squeezes the brass ring back into the

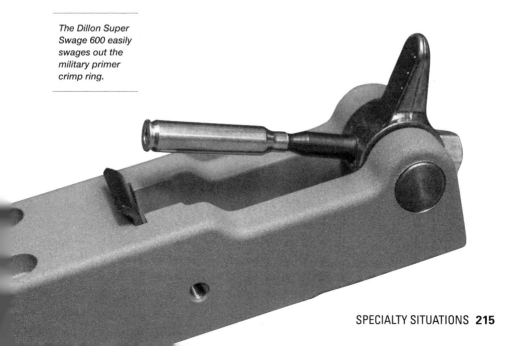

The Dillon Super Swage 600 easily swages out the military primer crimp ring.

case head, with little or no problem at all. Some swaging tools mount to the press and use the leverage of the press to squeeze out that crimp. My favorite tool for swaging military brass primer pockets is a separate bench-mounted device. The RCBS Bench Mount Primer Pocket Swager is a fine tool, but my particular tool of choice is the Dillon Super Swage 600. The simple little unit uses leverage to swage that crimp right out of your hair and works quickly and effectively. Either tool is available in the small primer pocket size (for .223/5.56mm) and the large primer pocket size (for .308/7.62mm NATO and the .30-06 Springfield).

Once the brass is clean and well inspected and the primer crimp is removed, you must look still further at

Hodgdon's H335 is a great choice for .223 Remington/5.556mm loading in the military-style rifles.

the primer pocket. Now you're looking for excess primer sealant, which must be scraped out, as well as a flash hole that is burred and has metal protruding into the primer pocket. You see, most military brass has a punched flash hole, unlike sporting brass cases, which have a reamed flash hole. When a flash hole gets punched through the case web from the mouth, it sometimes leaves ragged brass in the primer pocket, so the primer pocket scraper is almost essential here, to remove excess sealant and also any bits of brass left over from the punching process. I would also at this time use a flash hole tool to true-up the hole and ensure you have a concentric flash hole for perfect ignition.

Now onto the first issue with military brass, it's thicker walls. The outside dimensions of the cartridge case, even in military brass, must be held to the same SAAMI specifications as the thinner sporting brass, but the thicker case walls of military brass reduce their case capacity. Because of this reduction in allowable volume, you must load with an appropriate reduction in your powder charge. Generally, a 10-percent reduction should work out just fine, but an even better idea would be to consult a reloading manual that produced its test data using military brass. The *Speer Reloading Manual No. 13* (which is a manual I consult often), used Israeli Military cases for its test data in both the .223 Remington and .308 Winchester listings. Such sets of data would, therefore, require no reduction.

Another consideration. The semi-automatic action of the popular

Redding .308 Winchester bushing dies. (Photos both pages courtesy Massaro Media Group & J.D. Fielding Photography)

military-style rifles that we sportsmen and -women enjoy can be rather harsh on ammunition, especially during the phase in which the cartridge is picked up from the rifle's magazine and delivered into the chamber for the next squeeze of the trigger. This action treats the unfired cartridge much like the inertia hammer does when you are trying to pull bullets out of a case. The *Sierra Rifle & Handgun Reloading Data, Edition V* tells the tale of bullets being pulled out of their cases between 0.002-inch and 0.007-inch during loading from magazine to chamber. This can *dramatically* affect accuracy. A crimp on the case mouth *could* help prevent that bullet from moving, but putting a crimp on a bullet that has no cannelure is never a good idea. Sierra

recommends using a Redding bushing die, so I grabbed the telephone and gave my pal Robin Sharpless at Redding a jingle, to further discuss this issue.

The goal is to have the best neck tension possible on the bullet, to hold it in place during the cycling process. What Robin told me the bushing dies provide is a series of bushings, in 0.002-inch increments, which do *not* overwork the neck portion of the brass any more than is absolutely necessary. After measuring the outside dimension of the brass you intend to use with a bullet installed, the bushing of an appropriate size in installed in the die and, upon resizing, the case neck is squeezed down a minimum dimension before being worked over the expander ball. This process allows the brass in the neck portion of the case to live longer.

By not overworking the neck (because it is a thicker military case wall in a conventional die), you will get a longer case life and the brass will remain concentric longer. Better concentricity equals better neck tension and, therefore, reduces the amount of the "inertia hammer" effect. Sharpless knows of what he speaks. I also believe that, when resizing brass, military or otherwise, for the auto-loading military-style rifles, you should be using a small-base resizing die. The small-base dies will resize the case completely, all the way to the base, to prevent any jams in your auto-loading rifles. This is a good thing. Jams are awful.

Another thing to consider is that many of the military rifles your cases are loaded for use a firing pin that protrudes during the loading process and, as violent as the cycling is, your ammunition should use a primer that is of military specification. The CCI No. 34 Large Rifle primer and the CCI No. 41 Small Rifle primer have much harder cups than their sporting counterparts (the CCI 200 and CCI 400, respectively), and are designed for this application. I believe these harder primers greatly reduce the chance of a slam-fire (an accidental firing when the rifle goes into battery). These primers have a magnum

RCBS Small Base dies for the .223 Remington.
(Photos both pages courtesy Massaro Media Group & J.D. Fielding Photography)

A .45-120 Sharps case waiting in the loading block for blackpowder to be dropped through the brass tube.

primer spark, yet should be fine for all military rifle applications.

BLACKPOWDER CARTRIDGES

Our classic lever-action and single-shot cartridges were originally loaded with blackpowder. They can still be loaded that way. However, handling and loading blackpowder requires an *entirely* different mindset, as well as some special loading techniques.

The loading of blackpowder cartridges is a small world unto itself, and entire volumes have been written on the subject. I'll do my best to enlighten you on process, but I highly suggest you do all the research you can and ask many questions before you start. These procedures are finicky, and they require both different

tools and more experimentation than does loading with smokeless powder.

Unlike smokeless powder, the BATFE classifies blackpowder as an explosive. It burns much faster than any smokeless powder and is susceptible to reaction with static electricity. Therefore you should *never* use any plastic measuring device with blackpowder. All the tools used for handling blackpowder should be made from brass, although, oddly, I've seen aluminum products pop up for sale by major manufacturers. That aside, I like to stick to brass components, as they have been used safely for well more than 100 years.

Modern blackpowder substitutes like Triple Seven, Pyrodex, or American Pioneer are all loaded in the same

The brass drop tube, used to load blackpowder cartridges.

manner as true blackpowder. However, the after-shooting gun cleanup is a whole lot easier with the substitutes. Either way, all of them clean up with soap and hot water (and a bunch of elbow grease), and the sooner you clean after shooting your firearm, the better off you'll be. Blackpowder is very corrosive, both real and substitute, and will both make a mess of the bore and eat up your brass cases if left unclean.

Choosing a primer for a blackpowder case is a bit of a process. Some of the smaller cases (say .40-caliber and below), can use a Large Pistol primer in lieu of a rifle primer. The smaller spark is still sufficient to ignite the charge of very fast burning blackpowder. There is also some discussion of the pistol primer actually improving accuracy, as the lighter spark moves the powder column less upon ignition than a hotter spark from a rifle primer or magnum rifle primer would. I can't attest to an actual improvement in my rifles, but I know enough to listen to the masters in this field. As you get into the bigger cases and larger powder charges, the rifle primer will certainly come into play. Again, read the books on this topic to become the most proficient.

Now, unlike their smokeless powder fueled counterparts, blackpowder cartridges have their charges measured by volume, instead of weight. The goal is to load the case with a slight compression of the blackpowder, so that there is no air space in the case.

The powder is loaded into the case with a brass drop tube, usually one about 24 inches long, that length needed to achieve a more uniform compression. Again, the use of all-brass loading components is very important to eliminating the chance of a static electric charge developing.

In a bottleneck cartridge, like the .30-30 WCF, .32 Winchester Special, or the .38-56 Winchester, the powder is filled to a point about halfway up the case neck and the bullet is then installed to give $1/16$- or $1/8$-inch of powder compression. Filler wads cut to the specific diameter appropriate to the cartridge are installed at the base of the bullet, to give uniform compression and to help reduce lead fouling in the gun's bore by preventing the burning powder from melting the lead at the base of the bullet. These wads can be made of vegetable fiber (available from most retailers who sell reloading components), or punched from milk carton material. It is very important that, when you load a bottlenecked blackpowder cartridge, you do not seat the bullet too deeply, otherwise the wads will fall below the case neck and you'll lose all that uniformity.

When you load for the straight-walled blackpowder cartridges like the .38-55 Winchester or the ultra popular .45-70 Government, the same case flaring and crimping techniques will apply that you use in a straight-wall smokeless powder loading. You'll want to measure the amount of powder needed in the case to give the necessary level of compression, again, $1/16$- or $1/8$-inch once the bullet is seated in the case. If you want to reduce the load, either because of a lack of accuracy or a surplus of recoil, the space can be (carefully) filled with a specially made material called Puff-Lon. This substance is specifically made for the filling of extra space in blackpowder and other cartridges. I've read of folks using Dacron, cotton balls, and even dry, uncooked Cream of Wheat cereal to fill up the case, but I do not recommend using anything other than Puff-Lon.

To obtain proper compression of your blackpowder load, use a compression die instead of using the bullet to compress the powder upon seating. The results are well worth the extra step. Bullet seating in the lever-action rifles, for instance, dictates that you must adhere to the COL of the published cartridge, but, in the single-shot Sharps-style rifles, you can experiment with seating depth and COL. *Never* let the bullet touch the lands of the rifling, in order to keep pressures safe, but you can get close to them if that gives better accuracy in your rifle.

Whether to use FFg or FFFg will depend on the cartridge you are loading. The blackpowder cases of .30- to .40-calibers usually like to use FFFg, and the bigger cases can effectively use FFg. I know some blackpowder shooters who use Fg (usually classified as a cannon or musket powder), in the big .45-120 and .50-140. The brand of powder is also a personal choice, but some powders have different loading recommendations. Goex, Swiss, Elephant, and Schuetzen are all reputable brands that have delivered consistent results to blackpowder shooters for many years.

Bullets for blackpowder metallic loading should be of soft lead and coated with a bullet lube to keep the lead fouling soft inside the bore. Many blackpowder shooters use a blow tube to deliver moist breath into the bore between shots, as the humidity will soften lead fouling. This tube is especially handy when shooting in a very dry climate, as lead fouling becomes a problem much sooner. Soft (moist) fouling is okay for a while, but hard fouling will affect accuracy much sooner.

The .300 Winchester Magnum and its short neck.

(Photos both pages courtesy Massaro Media Group & J.D. Fielding Photography)

The author's neighbor Dave and his .350 Remington Magnum.

SHORT NECKS AND LONG BULLETS

There are a few situations you'll run into while loading, where the SAAMI-specified COL won't allow you to load certain bullets with a long ogive. A couple examples come quickly to mind in the .300 Winchester Magnum and the .350 Remington Magnum.

When Winchester developed its .300 Magnum, it used the basic formula that had worked so well with the .264, .338, and .458. It took the .375 H&H case, shortened it to fit in a standard long-action (.30-06-length) receiver, and necked it to hold the appropriate diameter bullet. Well, when the fourth in the series appeared, everyone expected it to have the same case length as the predecessors, 2.500 inches, but Winchester fooled

everyone. What it did was move the shoulder further forward, which gave the case a length of 2.620 inches. This still allowed it to fit in the long-action, but gave additional case capacity. It also left it with a neck length of 0.264-inch, which doesn't sit well with some folks, being less than one caliber in length; it's purported the neck doesn't give proper tension. I've never had an issue with that, but, what this new configuration did leave us with was very little room between the case mouth and the maximum COL.

If you have a new long-range bullet with a sleek secant ogive, you may have an issue. Problem is, if you load that bullet to the maximum COL listed by SAAMI, the short neck portion of the case will be sitting on the curved ogive of the long bullet, rather than the

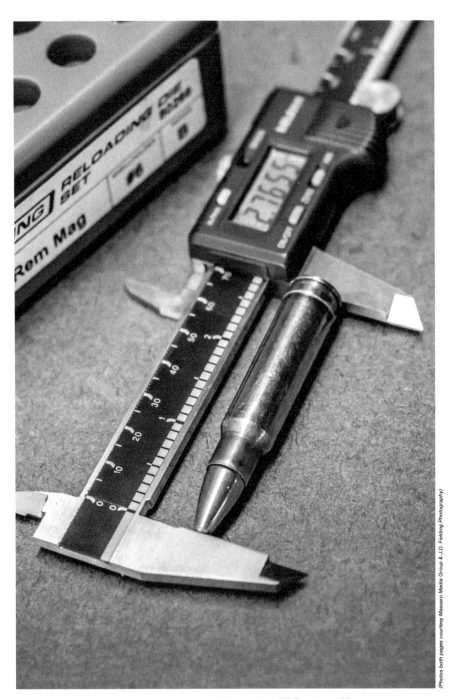

The shorter .35-caliber bullets work very well with the stubby .350 Remington Magnum.

The longer .358-inch diameter bullets can't be used in the short .350 Remington Magnum case, as the case mouth cannot seat on the bullet ogive.

parallel sides of the bullet. This situation is dangerous, because the bullet can actually fall into the case without enough neck tension on the bullet. The same concept applies to the .350 Remington Magnum, as its COL is limited by the magazine length.

If it is a single-shot rifle and the bullet does *not* come in contact with the lands and grooves, it is perfectly acceptable to seat bullets out past the SAAMI maximum dimension, but, in a bolt-action magazine rifle, you are limited to magazine length. There are bullet companies that have come to the rescue, such as Nosler, which recognized this problem, especially in the .300, and produced its famous Partition bullet with a "Protected Point." In this, Nosler rounded the nose slightly, allowing the handloader to move the bullet forward and ensure that the proper neck tension was produced, thus eliminating all chances of the bullet falling into the case.

With the .350 Remington case, I've found I have to stay away from some of the longer, sleeker bullets and stick with the round-nose and semi-spitzer bullets. A particular test rifle I use from time to time is my neighbor Dave's Remington 700 Classic, because we gain a bit of room in the magazine length over the traditional Remington Model 7 that is normally chambered for this cartridge. The dilemma is a little different with this one, in that, when we maintain the maximum COL the magazine will allow, the longest 250-grain spitzers in .358-inch caliber will sit so deep into the cartridge case, the case mouth is well into the bullet ogive and the bullet can fall into the case and, even if it didn't, there wouldn't be enough case capacity to attain proper velocity. In this particular case, we want to use bullets that keep their weight forward and their shape more rounded. North Fork 225-grainers, Hornady 200- and 250-grain Interlocks, and other bullets of similar shape and style will help you find that perfect balance between case capacity, velocity, and overall length.

TWIST RATES AND ACCURACY

Sometimes you'll read about barrels or cartridges that won't stabilize certain bullets. The .308 Winchester, when it was introduced, had a twist rate of 1:12, that is, the rifling in the bore will make one complete revolution over 12 inches of barrel. When compared to the .30-06, which generally featured a 1:10 twist rate, the .308 Winchester with its slower rate of twist wouldn't stabilize the long, heavy 220-grain bullets. As a kid, I couldn't make sense of this. Why wouldn't it stabilize a bullet designed for the same bore dimension as the .30-06? Why would the designers develop a barrel that wouldn't work with all bullet weights within a certain caliber?

Ol' Grumpy Pants was such a proponent of the .308 Winchester (largely based upon his experience in the Army National Guard basic training, in 1968), he convinced me the .308 was more than sufficient for anything I would ever hunt. That didn't quell the burning curiosity of this young man—I simply *had* to know what I was missing.

It took a while, but I figured it out. The longer a bullet is, the faster it must be spun in order for it to arrive on target without turning sideways, or "keyholing." This term derives from the imprint made on a target when a bullet is no longer rotating on its long axis. Instead of making a perfect caliber-sized hole in the paper, it hits sideways (or radically off axis) and the tear is elongated, like a keyhole. The bottom line is that the .308's 1:12 twist rate doesn't spin the long, 220-grain bullets enough to hold them in an on-axis rotation. The .30-06, on the other hand, with its 1:10 twist, will stabilize them just fine. Understanding how twist works, then, with my .308 Winchester loads, I utilize (very well, I might add), the lighter-for-caliber bullets, those between 125 and 180 grains. Simply put, use the right tool for the right job.

This same issue was very detrimental to the early sales of the .244 Remington. The .244 was a .257 Roberts (or 7x57 Mauser case), necked down to hold 6mm bullets. The beauty of the 6mm cartridges is that they are capable of pulling double duty on both varmints and deer/antelope-sized game. The only issue was that the twist rate in the barrels for the .244 was 1:12. This twist worked very well with the lighter varmint-weight bullets, like the 55-, 60-, and 70-grain bullets, but would not work well with the deer/antelope-weight bullets, the larger 90-, 100-, and 105-grainers, because the twist rate was too slow.

The closest competition to the .244 Remington, the .243 Winchester, was based on the 51mm-long .308 Winchester case. When you compare the case capacity between the .244 Remington (with a 1:12 twist rate) and the .243 Winchester (with a 1:10 twist rate), the .244 is the clear winner. But the .243 Winchester is the more versatile of the two, because it would stabilize, although at a slower velocity, the bullets suitable for deer and antelope hunting.

Remington took *eight years* to correct the situation, revising the barrel twist from 1:12 to 1:9 and, eventually, renaming the cartridge the 6mm Remington. The new twist rate would stabilize any 6mm bullet within the realm of sanity, but, unfortunately for Remington, the rot had set in. The marketing world is a finicky thing,

The author's dad, ol' Grumpy Pants, is actually happy, when he has his .308 Winchester in hand.

and, by the time Remington revised the twist rate and name, the .243 Winchester had caught on like wildfire. This is why, among the 6mm cases, the .243 reigns supreme and some younger hunters haven't even heard of the larger cased .244 Remington.

What in blazes does this have to do with our task at hand? An awful lot. Don't try to drive nails with a screwdriver. In other words, if the reloading manual tells you a round requires a certain twist rate to stabilize a particularly long bullet, believe it and don't waste your time trying to disprove the data.

This kind of knowledge has great relevance in the AR platform that enjoys target-grade .223 bullets. I like the heavy-for-caliber 62- and 69-grain bullets, but they require a 1:10 and 1:9 minimum twists, respectively. If your barrel has a slower twist rate (1:12 or 1:16), these bullets are off-limits to you. Stick to the 45-, 50-, and 55-grain projectiles. Do the research and know your barrel's twist rate. It will save you a ton of time and money in trying to get your rifle to perform well.

Wait, how do you determine the twist rate of the rifle you own? Why, I thought you'd never ask! Take a cleaning rod with a freely rotating handle and a tight fitting patch, and insert it a couple inches into the bore. Place a piece of tape on the rod just ahead of the handle, place a mark on the very top of it, and measure the distance from the edge of the receiver to the front of the tape. Then insert the rod through the bore until that mark revolves around to the top of the rod. Measure the distance from the edge of receiver and subtract the two measurements. This gives you the exact amount of bore travel it takes to make one revolution. Boo-yah, you've got your rifles rate of twist! Of course, you could pick up the phone, call the manufacturer, read them the serial number, and ask them what they installed on the gun. Either way.

OH, THE NORTHEAST WOODS!

Where I hunt, in the woods of upstate New York, our primary big-game quarry is the whitetail deer. Unless you have access to wide-open farm fields or hunt the cut power line rights-of-way, your shots here will average less than 100 yards. We are permitted to hunt with a rifle in most of the Hudson Valley, as well as in the Catskill and Adirondack mountains that I love so much. There the woods are thick and getting thicker. The use of a rifle scope will give you an advantage, as it allows you to see the tiny branches and ends of limbs that might deflect your bullet.

As the ranges are relatively short in such a setting, the use of a boat-tail spitzer isn't necessarily needed, but please don't overlook the good old round-nosed bullets! They have several advantages, when the shots are on the closer end of the spectrum.

First, they keep the bullet weight forward, which means that a round-nosed bullet will be shorter than its spitzer counterpart. This will give more room within the case, so load density doesn't become an issue. Simply, the bullet takes up less of the case, so there's less need for a compressed load.

These are .30-caliber bullets, a flat-base round-nosed 220-grain (left) and a boat-tail spitzer.
(Photo courtesy Massaro Media Group & J.D. Fielding Photography)

Second, and this is purely my own observation, I believe that round-nosed bullets hit harder or, at least, they have a more pronounced impact on an animal. Many times, when I've hit a deer, bear, or whatever with a round-nosed bullet, I can see the animal shudder upon impact. That's certainly not to say that the spitzer bullets work less effectively, it's just that I feel that the additional meplat diameter of the round-nose bullets has a different hydraulic effect on game animals.

There's another theory, which, in my mind has some merit and at the very least deserves some further investigation. The good folks at North Fork and I had an interesting conversation about bullet meplat design and its effect on game. The results of that talk became the theory that a round-nosed bullet, with the weight held toward the frontal portion of the bullet (or at least more so than a spitzer or hollowpoint), will "pull" through the animal, much like the two wheels on a front-wheel-drive car pull their vehicle in a straight line. This gives the bullet deep penetration, often a complete pass-through. The hollowpoint or spitzer bullet, with its weight toward the rear of the bullet, will tend to "push" through the animal, like a rear-wheel-drive car, and tend to rotate or fish-tail once resistance has been met.

Now, it would take an extensive amount of well-controlled scientific research to either prove or disprove this theory, and the results could easily be debated for hours on end. Lacking that, what I do know is this: I like round-nosed bullets. After 200 yards, they can't hold a candle to their spitzer relations, as far as retained energy and velocity are concerned, but, within that distance, they are very impressive.

Think about our classic calibers like the .30-06 Springfield, 7x57 Mauser, .30-40 Krag, .30-30 WCF, and so on. They have *all* made their reputations on game with round-nosed bullets, and for good reason. They work! I can get them to shoot to at least MOA in my rifles, which is accurate enough to thread the needle in the Northeast woods, and I appreciate their performance on game. Give 'em a try!

THE .45 ACP: SMALL OR LARGE PRIMER POCKET?

There's a bunch of .45 ACP cartridges on the market that are using a small primer pocket and primer in lieu of the standard large pocket. Most of them utilize the lead-free or "non-toxic" priming compound, for use on indoor pistol ranges. The majority of common primers feature a small amount of lead in the priming compound, and the goal with many indoor shooting facilities today is to minimize airborne lead vapor by using bullets that are totally encapsulated with copper, as well as these Small Pistol non-toxic primers. I'm all about safety and not suffering the effects of lead poisoning, but it leaves us with the minor dilemma of dealing with .45 ACP brass having a different primer pocket sizes.

There is an inherent danger in trying to stuff a Large Pistol primer into a Small Pistol primer pocket, and that danger is primer detonation. If you

hand-prime all your pistol cases, the risk is more easily avoided, as the resistance will be felt immediately. But, if you use a press priming system, which has a huge mechanical advantage but less feel, the risk is much greater. Even worse, should a case with the small primer pocket get into the mix when using a progressive press, you risk the possibility of detonating multiple primers. This is definitely not a good thing and, in a small space and with powder in the dispenser, this is the kind of disaster you want to avoid at all costs.

The solution is to sort the daylights out of your brass. You really want to be certain that none of those cases with the small primer pockets are allowed to mingle with the other large pocket party guests. Segregate them and, if you choose to reload them, be sure and prime them separately. Keep them in a different container that's clearly marked, so as to avoid any and all confusion between the two types of brass. It is perfectly fine to load the brass with small primer pockets, using a Small Pistol primer and good load data, but safety is paramount.

HOT LOADS, DUDE

To me, it's like nails on a chalkboard. Invariably, someone will want to talk about reloading and the question spills forth from their lips like an uncontrollable belch: "Hey, man, can you make me some hot loads?" Um, no. Wait, let me double-check that for you. Yup, yeah, it's still no. Nope. No way.

The reloading manuals have established their pressure limits through rigorous testing, so there is no reason

"Ah call this the 'Massaro .057 Stinger'. It shoots a phonograph needle at half the speed of light."

There is such a
thing as too much
of a good thing.
*(Cartoon courtesy of
Bill Gaither)*

whatsoever to exceed it. Trying to push the envelope of safe pressures to attain higher velocities or energies or flatter trajectories puts your firearm and your current anatomical configuration in decided jeopardy. I've seen pistol shooters try to push the loads into the realm of "+P" (high-pressure factory loads), and have the results be cracked cylinders, broken grips, and so on. I've seen rifle shooters with loads that are way over maximum have their bolt-action guns lock up so tight-ly (a result of excessive pressures), that they needed to beat the bolt open with a mallet! There is no, none, *nada* logical reason to do this. If the cartridge you've chosen cannot deliver the ballistics you're looking for when loaded within safe parameters, you've chosen the wrong cartridge. A .30-06 Springfield isn't a .300 Weatherby, a .38 Special is not a .357 Magnum, and a .45 ACP can't be made to shoot like a .45 Colt. Don't think about it. Don't tinker with it. Just. Don't.

CHAPTER 10

SUCCESS STORIES

After all the diligent procedures have been followed and the proper combination of case, powder, primer, and bullet have been chosen, you head down the range and look at the target with pride, when you see a tiny little cloverleaf group you just put there. Joy!

Be it a varmint rifle, hunting revolver, carry pistol, deer rifle, or safari gun, the joy from a well-placed group on the target is a thing of beauty. You should be grinning from ear to ear! For you and for all the others like you, I'd like to dedicate this chapter to your success stories and hunting memories that have derived and will derive from diligent handloading.

THE LEARNING CURVE

When I was introduced to handloading, I latched onto more as a matter of economics than a desire for

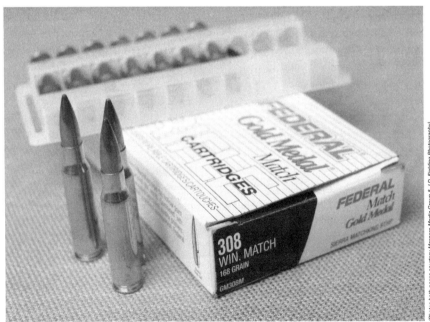

Federal Premium ammunition is a very well-made product, but, as a young man, it was out of the author's price range. He doesn't miss those days!

(Photos both pages courtesy Massaro Media Group & J.D. Fielding Photography)

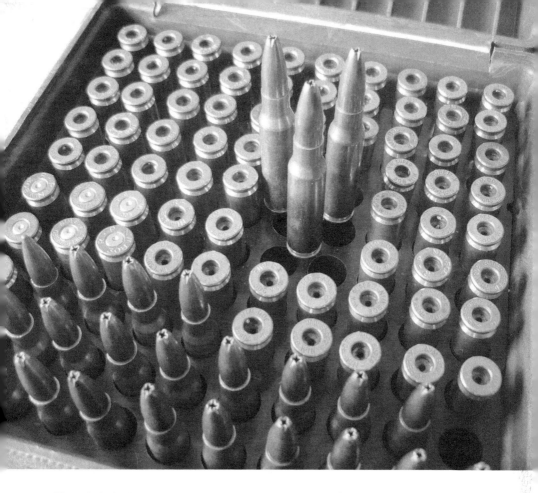

The author's dad insists on a 165-grain bullet over IMR4064 in his .308 Winchester loads. They don't suck, for the record.

supreme accuracy. Put bluntly, I didn't have a pot, let alone a window to toss it out of; a box of premium factory cartridges was very expensive for a 20-year-old hunter.

My Dad and I split the cost of some reloading gear and, as we both shot .308 Winchester bolt-action rifles for deer, spent some great time together developing a load that would suffice for both of us. We chose the 165-grain Hornady spire point, 43.5 grains of IMR4064 (Grumpy Pant's "official" powder—seriously, the guy ought to be sponsored), and a CCI200 Large Rifle primer. Both guns printed three-shot groups of about 1½ inches at 100 yards, which was perfectly good for the both of us. Many deer fell to those loads and many great memories were made in the deer woods—but then something happened.

I started reading about reloading. Our level of accuracy, at least to me, was unacceptable, and I had to start my load experimentation immediately! Ah, the beginnings of an addiction. I drove Dad insane on a daily basis with statistics on new powders, premium bullets, loading techniques, etc.

I simply couldn't get enough. I even had the audacity to leave behind the blessed combination of a 165-grain .308-inch bullet over IMR4064, much to GP's chagrin.

The first load I ever personally developed used the 125-grain Nosler Ballistic Tip and (gulp!) IMR4320. The only way I sold it to Dad was to prove to him that the factories used IMR4320 as fuel for the cartridges he used as a youth. That particular load still prints ¾-inch groups, and, although light-for-caliber, they kill very effectively, when properly placed. They are hell on both deer and coyotes. Approaching 3,000 fps, they are also very flat shooting. Imagine my pride, when I showed my dad I could develop a load all by my lonesome! This was awesome!

It was GP's turn next to break stride from the family .308 load. Whilst preparing for a caribou hunt in the northern reaches of Quebec, he wanted something that shot a bit flatter than the revered .308 Winchester. He couldn't quite leave the .30-caliber in and of itself behind (that would come some years later), and, so, chose the .300 Winchester Magnum.

After the first hunt, using his 165-grain bullets (which delivered mediocre accuracy, but ultimately yielded the caribou), I began to read. I discovered that the .300 was best served with 180-grain bullets. This discovery coincided with my thirtieth birthday, upon which I received mine own .300 Winchester as a birthday gift.

Once again, load development was done with my dad. We found that an appropriate load of Alliant's Reloder

19 and a Sierra 180-grain boat-tail gave wonderful accuracy, and it was with this load that I took my first head of "exotic" big game: a caribou bull, in Quebec, dad alongside me. Good times, for sure!

Developing a load for your firearm is a process of trial and error. There are nearly infinite combinations of primer/case/powder/bullet, and having your own unique load is part of the fun. Many times a rifle or handgun will like more than one load, and I often have on hand three or four different loads, each using different combinations, for my firearms. Start at the low end of the scale within the manual, work up slowly and, odds are, you'll eventually find the combination to provide the accuracy and velocities you're looking for.

AN AFRICAN CLASSIC

Throughout this book I've mentioned my .375 H&H Magnum. It is a push-feed, post-'64 Winchester Model 70. I've spent an awful lot of time behind the trigger of that rifle, first because it had a structural issue and I couldn't get it to shoot properly, and, second because I just simply loved it by the time I did get it to shoot right. I took that .375 with me on that aforementioned caribou hunt, because I just had to test it (it worked just fine). I also lent it out to GP for his first safari to South Africa. I built him a load around the 250-grain Sierra boat-tail GameKing, with a charge of IMR4350 sparked by a Federal Magnum Rifle primer, and got that big gun to shoot well under one inch. Dad had a great safari, taking both a 39-inch gemsbok and a 53-inch kudu on the same day. The bullet was a good choice for African plains game, and to say I was both honored and proud that Dad took my rifle and my handloads on safari is an understatement.

My own safari was to come two years later, and I brought both the .300 and the .375 across the pond. I was jonesin' for an eland, the largest African antelope, one that can weigh up to a ton. That's an awful lot of antelope! I cooked up a load using the 300-grain Swift A-Frame in my .375 H&H, and this load shot so well, it would be pretty much the only formula I would use in this rifle for a decade. I still shoot it.

Well, long story short, the only shot my eland bull would present me was one at 400 yards, though at least it was over very open ground. It was the preparation for this safari and the time spent at both the reloading bench and the shooting bench that allowed me to make that shot, the longest I've made to date. I'd printed ¾-inch groups with that bullet and chronographed the load, so I knew the trajectory very well. I'd zeroed the rifle to be dead on at 200 yards and prepared a drop chart on a laminated card, so I would know the drop out to 400 yards, which I imagined was well past the limits of my shooting. With a bit of encouragement from my Professional Hunter, who had seen me shoot for almost a week by the time the shot on the eland came, I leaned the old girl against a termite mound, in the prone position, held for the appropriate amount of holdover, and adjusted for the crosswind.

When the sound of the bullet hitting the shoulder bone of that big

bull drifted back on the wind, I began jumping up and down like a man who'd just won the lottery! Ecstatic, overjoyed, proud, and euphoric would all be adjectives applicable to that moment. The PH was equally jazzed, proclaiming, "I'd really hoped you'd make that shot!" Later he confessed he'd never have taken it himself—rascal! Point is, without having developed that load personally, putting it through the chronograph, and spending the time at the bench learning how the cartridge performed, I never, *ever* would have even attempted that shot. Nonetheless, that beautiful eland bull sits with pride in my trophy room, preserved eternally as a pedestal mount, and holds a place of honor among my hunting trophies.

You know what the really cool thing about that hunt was? The .375 H&H is not considered a long-range cartridge by any means, but, through handloading, I connected on the longest shot I've ever attempted. That rifle has three loads that work well at distance using 235-grain Barnes TSX bullets, Sierra 250-grain spitzer boat-

The author's big eland bull that fell to the 300-grain Swift A-Frame, in South Africa, in 2004. (Author Photo)

The long-barreled Ruger Blackhawk on the sandbag.

tails, and 300-grain Swift A-Frames or Hornady Solids. It's a pretty versatile setup, if you ask me.

WHEELGUNS ARE WONDERFUL!

It wasn't long after this safari that I received my pistol permit, the acquisi-tion of which is a lengthy process here in New York. I immediately drove to my local gun shop and ordered what I considered to be a really cool revolver, a Ruger Blackhawk chambered in .45 (Long) Colt, with a stainless finish, 7½-inch barrel, and adjustable sights. This is a *fetchin'* iron!

(Photo courtesy Massaro Media Group & J.D. Fielding Photography)

The factory loads I purchased had 255-grain lead bullets, but didn't impress me with their accuracy—I knew I could do better with that long barrel and adjustable sights to work with.

It was my intention to carry this wheelgun as a sidearm on my hunts in the Adirondacks, where a healthy population of bears exists. I wanted a heavy, stiff bullet that would get me out of trouble with a black bear, one that was accurate enough to place itself where it needed to go (provided I did my part, of course). I settled on the 300-grain Hornady XTP bullet. Then I read an article in the *Nosler Manual No. 4*, writ-

The author's .45 Colt loves 300-grain Hornady XTPs and 255-grain cast lead bullets, but it was handloading that got him to that level of affection.
(Photo courtesy Massaro Media Group & J.D. Fielding Photography)

ten by none other than Hank Williams, Jr., indicating that the .45 Colt liked to be fueled by Alliant's Unique powder, so I topped that XTP with a Large Pistol Magnum primer and a liberal dose of Unique stuffed into a Starline case and, after load development, was printing impressive groups with the hand-cannon. Turns out that Hank Junior was spot on with his powder choice.

Although Unique tends to burn a bit on the dirty side, I don't mind the cleaning chore, when the pistol will ring steel out to 75 yards with my aging eyes. It's great to get together with friends and show them what this gun is capable of, and, as a sidearm in the northern woods, I feel very confident about staying alive, should a bear pose a problem while hiking, camping, or otherwise. Later, I bought a bunch of those 255-grain cast lead bullets that the factory ammunition was loaded with and, with a different charge

weight of Unique, also got them to shoot quite accurately. They make an economical choice for practicing with my Ruger revolver, whether plinking or target shooting.

SMALLBORE SUCCESS

In the 1990s, the coyote population in upstate New York exploded. Sightings during deer season had become common. With an overdose of deer predation looming, the State placed a season on coyotes from October through March. We routinely shot 'yotes during deer season as opportunities presented themselves, but soon we began actively pursuing them to extend our time afield. My .308 Winchester worked fine for this, and I noticed that the coyotes were none too dead, but pelt damage was severe. Not really needing an excuse to purchase another rifle, I perused the loading manuals and settled on the .22-250

The author's favorite varmint rig, a Ruger Model 77 MkII in .22-250 Remington, with a Hogue over-molded stock and a Leupold Vari-X III 6.5-20x40mm AO scope.

Remington. Flat-shooting, minimally recoiling, and with a reputation for hair-splitting accuracy, I felt this would be the coyote gun for me.

I've been very happy with that choice. I ordered a Ruger Model 77 Mark II with a sporting-contour barrel and topped it with a Leupold Vari-X III 6.5-20x40mm scope that has an adjustable objective lens. It's a serious varmint rig, right there, gotta tell you.

In hindsight, I probably should have ordered the rifle with a bull barrel, to avoid barrel heat buildup, but I'll get to that in a minute. The initial load I developed used the Winchester 55-grain FMJ over IMR4320, travelling at 3,350 fps. Group size is usually around ¾-inch, and while that load is fine for coyotes and foxes, I knew the

gun could do better, but I still had one issue with the hardware: The trigger Ruger put in the Mk II broke at about six pounds. In the inimitable words of Pink Floyd, "This shall not do." A quick phone call to Timney Triggers solved the dilemma. In fact, a replacement trigger was such an improvement over the factory version that the groups were cut in *half*.

Now, in my quest for accuracy, I discovered there was a powder that went hand in hand with the .22-250 Remington, Hodgdon's H380. This powder was a WWII military surplus powder that Bruce Hodgdon fell deeply in love with, so deep, in fact, that he named the powder after his pet load: 38.0 grains under a 55-grain bullet. So H380 was born, and I am here to testify that this powder works very, *very* well in this case. I started with Mr. H's chosen load, but it needed some tweaking in my gun, so I prepared groups of three cartridges with powder charges that varied, up and down, by 0.1-grain. It didn't take long before I found what I was looking for. My own pet load for my .22-250 is 38.4 grains of H380 over a 53-grain Sierra Match-King flat-base hollowpoint. Group size averaged $^3/_8$-inch and the round travelled at 3,550 fps. Coyotes and foxes fell like the French Army.

THE HANDLOADERS SYNDICATE

Let us fast forward, with the same rifle in mind, to a friendly handloaders' competition. The best handloaders in my area congregated at our local brew pub and, upon conclusion of some two and half hours of semi-intelligent discussion, we had settled upon a date, time, and place to have a shooting competition. Those in the know would gather their accoutrements, their prized rifles, the best handloads they believed they could produce, and congregate to test their various mettles. The competition was divided into two classes: Smallbore (.17-caliber through 6.5mm) and large-bore (.277-caliber through .375). The range would be 200 yards, with three-shot groups from a benchrest, on a beautiful September Saturday.

I brought the .22-250 along for the smallbore competition, to be placed in the battle next to a .223 and .243, both in Remington 700s with full one-inch pipes, and a Weatherby Vanguard Sub-MOA in .257 Weatherby Magnum. Nothing was at

The Handloaders Syndicate: a meeting of the minds.

(Photos both pages courtesy Massaro Media Group & J.D. Fielding Photography)

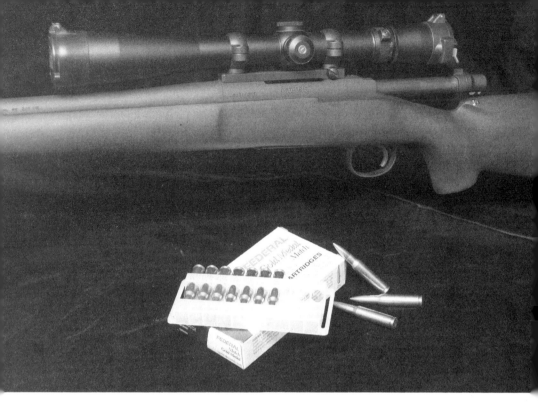

Pig-Newton's sweetheart .308, a Remington Model 700 Police Special, with Leupold scope and McMillan stock. It is deadly accurate.

stake but my bragging rights among my peers and some dignity, so I'd prepared the best of the best, using Norma cases, Federal match-grade primers, and my own developed load based on H380. I hand-trimmed the cases, weighed out the Sierra Match-King projectiles, and did my best to cobble together the components.

It worked. The .223 fell victim to my handloads first, and then the .257 Weatherby. My pals couldn't believe the sporter-weight barrel was shooting better groups than the bull barrels and specialty rifles. Even the .243 fell, though it didn't go down easily, as the shooter was a worthy adversary, but, in the end, the pencil-barreled .22-250 reigned supreme.

Damned fine handloading, and a bit of decent shooting on my part, led to the "championship."

That same good loading technique came back to bite me in the bottom in the large-bore competition. Well, sort of. I'd sold my good friend and neighbor Dave DeMoulpied a 1959 Colt Coltsman chambered in .300 Holland & Holland and helped him develop the load. We used Reloder 22 powder, a Federal GM215M primer, and the Swift Scirocco 180-grain bullet. When we tried out the load on the range the day before the shoot, Dave printed a 1.2-inch group at 200 yards, aiming through a 9x hunting scope. I had serious competition, as I knew my buddy Mark "Pig Newton"

Nazi was bringing his Remington 700 Police Special in .308 Winchester and, between those two rifles, it would take everything I had to remain competitive. Mark's .308, with its bull barrel, would routinely print less than ½-MOA. My .300 Winchester was good, but the field was tough.

In the end, neighbor Dave put me out of the running, when I admittedly pulled the third shot of my group and, so, it came down to the other two rifles for the championship. Pig Newton beat Dave, but it took the micrometer to prove it. Either way, there was something to be said for both the guns, especially the accuracy of the .300 H&H in a hunting-grade rifle. I didn't win the large-bore trophy, but I'd helped a friend develop a crazy-accurate hunting load! To me, we'd all won—but I never should have sold that rifle.

GO BIG OR GO HOME

At the meeting of our local chapter of SCI, in Oneonta, New York, something happened to me that never, ever happens. I won a raffle. A raffle for a rifle! Well, at least money toward any rifle I wanted. I had a .22-250 Remington, .308 Winchester, .300 Winchester Magnum, and a .375 Holland & Holland. So what to order.

I thought long and hard about a .25-06 Remington, but my love for big-bore rifles ultimately won out and I ordered a Winchester Model 70 in .416 Remington Magnum. I had aspirations to hunt Cape buffalo, a beast affectionately known as the Black Death. These brutal bovines have a reputation for soaking up copious amounts of lead, so, as a hunter, you want to hit them hard. I really don't believe there's a rifle that is too large

The champions of the Handloader's Syndicate, left to right, Mark "Pig-Newton" Nazi, large-bore champ, and yours truly, the smallbore champ.

(Photos both pages courtesy Massaro Media Group & J.D. Fielding Photography)

for these buffalo, *so long as you can put the bullet in the vitals.* Shot placement is paramount—they're just not gonna die from an "okay" shot.

I'd spent some time loading the .458 Winchester with this quest in mind, but its case capacity and recoil were two factors I wasn't a huge fan of, so the .416 Remington kind of leapt out at me. It burns about 75 percent of the powder the .416 Rigby does, while delivering identical ballistics. The parent case is the .375 H&H, which is readily available in a pinch,

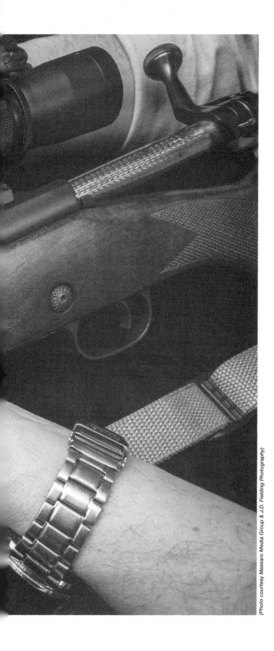

"Cocoa," the author's beloved Winchester Model 70 in .416 Remington Magnum. The Leupold QR mounts allow quick access to the iron sights, if they are needed.

and the Winchester 70 platform is well known to me. I saw no point in loading anything less than the 400-grain bullets, as these made the .416's reputation, plus, I already had a .375 H&H for throwing 300-grain bullets at other game. As I was going to use this rifle for buffalo, I chose a low-powered 1.5-5x20mm Leupold VXIII with a heavy duplex and mounted it in Leupold QR mounts. These mounts would easily give me access to the rifle's iron sights, and the scope has enough magnification to make longer

The author and his .416 Remington at the bench.

shots, if necessary. The initial setup complete, it was now off to the reloading bench to start load development.

I chose a trio of bullets to use, the Hornady 400-grain round-nosed Interlock for practice and smaller animals, and a combination of 400-grain Swift A-Frames and Hornady round-nosed solids for the buffalo. Some nickel-plated Remington cases were handed over by the UPS man, and I reached for the Federal 215 primers and Grumpy Pant's favorite powder, IMR4064.

The first loading through the brand new barrel printed three-shot groups of just over two inches, which, as GP indicated, would have been well suited for

100 yds.
.416 Rem
400 Gr. Swift
1.0" group
2,405 fps

(Photos this page courtesy Massaro Media Group & J.D. Fielding Photography)

A one-inch group from the author's .416 Remington, not too shabby from a 5x scope and a big-bore rifle.

A nice Chobe bushbuck taken with a 400-grain Swift a-Frame, in Zambia.

buffalo hunting, as shots on them are rarely over 100 yards and the buffalo's vitals very large. But why would I ever settle for that level of accuracy, when I had the capability of loading the ammunition to give better results?

Back at the bench, I changed the amount of IMR4064 in the case by one grain, up to an even 78.0 grains, which was near maximum, according to the reloading manuals. Four groups of three shots verified that I had no signs of excessive pressure, and the accuracy was much better. Group size averaged 0.9-inch, which, with a 5x scope, is just fine by me.

The chronograph displayed 2,405 fps, on par with factory ammunition. I was initially skeptical about the Leupold QR mounts and the claim of being able to remove the scope from the rifle and reinstall it without losing zero. Well, turns out they work and work well. In fact, they work so well, they sparked an idea.

I've had scopes fail on a remote hunt before. When that happens, more often than not, you're out of business. Now, on this rifle, destined for Africa, I could remove the scope if it broke and use the iron sights, but I thought that purchasing an extra set of rings and a spare scope, one already zeroed and carried in my day pack, would save any aggravation. So, in addition to the 1.5-5x, I picked up a fixed 2.5x Leupold and zeroed it to use as my spare. This has worked perfectly, and though I haven't had any issues with the main scope, I'm ready if there's a problem. The ammunition, too, worked perfect in Africa, and, in fact,

The author with a large Zambian Cape buffalo bull, taken with his .416 Remington Magnum.
(Photo courtesy Massaro Media Group & J.D. Fielding Photography)

this rifle has accompanied me across the pond twice, on safaris to Tanzania and Zambia. It accounted for my first Cape buffalo, a 36-inch-wide bull with a huge body and well-worn and hardened bosses. The bull required only one shot, one placed right through the heart, but my PH insisted I "pay the insurance" with a second A-Frame. Both bullets were recovered against the offside skin and retained more than 90 percent of their initial weight. This same ammunition also allowed me to take a rare Lichtenstein's hartebeest, in Tanzania's Selous Reserve, at 300 yards across a large pan of water. Once again, the laminated drop chart card came into play and allowed me to take a longer than normal shot with the big gun.

This is, without a doubt, my favorite safari rifle, especially for truly big game, but I've also used it on warthog, bushbuck, puku (another rarity), and on a wild hog here in the States. The other nice feature of this rifle is that all three of the bullets I choose to load in it will print to very nearly the same point of impact. I really couldn't be happier with this rifle!

MAMA NEEDS A RIFLE

After our safari to Zambia, my darling wife, Suzie, decided she wanted to start to hunt and shoot with me. Absolutely! I couldn't wait to spend time afield with my best friend, even though it cost me almost half my hunting gear.

Now, I'm almost six feet tall, but my dear bride is only all of three inches more than five feet, so most of my rifles and shotguns don't suit her

well. I needed to get her a rifle that was better stocked to her dimensions. While at the Harrisburg, Pennsylvania, annual outdoor sportsmen's show, I had a visit and a chat with the folks from Savage Arms. They told me about a new development in their lineup, the Savage Lady Hunter. It has the same great barreled action that Savage has always produced, but with a scaled down instead of cut down stock. This is a huge advantage for Suzie Q, as she has strong yet small hands and requires a much shorter length of pull than any of my big-game rifles can offer her.

When I saw the Lady Hunter, I knew what Mrs. Massaro was going to receive for her birthday, but I debated long and hard about the choice of calibers. I knew that it would have to be relatively universal, as Mama had indicated she didn't want a bunch of different rifles (silly girl), but also that she had aspirations to hunt both the game of North America and the African antelopes, especially sable. I figured a .30-caliber would fit the bill, but had to choose between .308 Winchester and the venerable .30-06 Springfield. Since the rifle would already be scaled down and feature a shorter barrel, I reasoned that the .308 Winchester would give a lighter overall package (due to a shorter receiver), and still perform well in the shorter tube. I also had plenty of component brass and some good loads developed for my own .308, so the shorter cartridge was the way to go.

When the rifle arrived, I was very pleased with the walnut stock; nice grain, a decent wood-to-metal fit, and that awesome Savage barrel. Mama

Suzie Q at the bench with her Savage Lady Hunter in .308 Winchester.

picked out a Bushnell 3-9x scope that was lying around, so I mounted it on her rifle and we were off to the range. The barrel break-in stage showed that accuracy was not going to be an issue, as the loads I'd developed for GP's rifle worked well in Suzie's, giving her about 1 MOA. Indeed, my wife shot her rifle well right out of the gate and she soon used her fetchin' iron to take a big, black, wild boar in Florida, with a 165-grain Nosler Partition and an appropriate load of IMR4064. Then something happened that really showed the true accuracy potential of this rig.

My pal Ronnie Hardy, owner of Hardy's Custom Calls and an avid hunter, called me to develop him a load for his T/C Icon in .308 Winchester. He had asked for a flat-shooting 150-grain bullet to reach out

and touch a large Canadian whitetail. I decided to use Suzie's rifle to develop the load. I trimmed up some Hornady Match brass, weighed out some 150-grain Swift Sciroccos, grabbed some Federal Gold Medal Large Rifle Match primers, and cobbled them together with (yet again) IMR4064.

I thought the first three-shot group was a fluke, as I watched the single hole in the target just get wider—*0.3-inch wide* from center to center, to be precise.

"Gimme three more. That had to be a coincidence."

The second group printed 0.35-inch, the third the same. Wow, just *wow*. The chronograph gave an average of 2,865 fps, something that would certainly give the trajectory Ronnie was looking for. I made him a couple boxes and sent them out. A phone call later that week confirmed

A very good group from the Suzie Massaro's .308. You really can't ask for more than that from a hunting rifle. (Photos both pages courtesy Massaro Media Group & J.D. Fielding Photography)

Suzie's chosen load for her pet rifle is a .308-inch, 150-grain Swift Scirocco II loaded in Lapua cases.

that his rifle had liked them as much as Suzie's had. He's since taken many deer with that gun and load.

It's wonderful to introduce new shooters to the sport, and, if you have plans of taking your significant other or children to the range, you can make some handloads that are on the lighter end of the spectrum, so that harsh recoil won't create bad shooting habits. I made some of these reduced-velocity loads for Suzie, so she could get comfortably acquainted with the way her rifle shot, the feel of the trigger, and use of the safety. It wasn't long until she had developed a good shooting technique, and those skills stuck with her when we switched to the full-house loads for hunting big game.

A BIG THIRTY WITH AN ATTITUDE PROBLEM

The late 1990s saw the release of a case based on a blown out .404

Jeffrey, one with near parallel sides and necked down to hold .308-inch diameter bullets. That round was the .300 Remington Ultra Magnum. It was among the first cases to have the "magnum" moniker, without having the raised belt of brass associated with the .375 Holland & Holland Magnum. This round is capable of driving a 180-grain bullet at velocities past 3,300 fps, which gives it a very flat trajectory, and it produces more than 4,000 ft-lbs of energy at the muzzle.

My friend Pieter had a Remington Alaskan Wilderness Rifle chambered for this cartridge, topping the gun with a Swarovski high-magnification rifle scope with the TDS reticle, a very useful setup for long-range shooting. Pieter is a very good shot and an experienced hunter who knows his rifle very well. This big stick liked factory ammunition using the 180-grain Nosler Partition. However, with the great ammo crunch of 2013, factory ammunition was simply unavailable at any price. Pieter had tried several different lots of handloaded ammunition, but none of them came close to giving the accuracy his factory loads had given him. He gave me a call to see if I could solve the problem.

I had developed the load that my dad uses for his .300 RUM, so I had a good idea where to start. I first made Pete a couple of loads on the lower end of the spectrum, to check for pressure signs. We had none, and the accuracy started to tighten up, but we weren't where we wanted to be yet. Pete uses this rifle for long-range elk hunting out west, so we had to have accuracy somewhere below MOA, to be sure and he could make clean hits on distant targets.

As we worked through the loads, barrel heat was a bit of an issue, thanks to the bullets moving at this velocity, so we kept the groups to three shots. We were getting close to the accuracy we wanted with the 180-grain Swift Scirocco II and Reloder 25 powder backed by a Federal 215 Large Rifle Magnum primer, that combination yielding around 1 MOA. Still, I knew we could do better, so I pulled out the old neck-sizing die, resizing the necks only on Pete's once-fired brass. That did the trick. Three shot groups hovered around ⁵/₈-inch, with velocities around 3,350 fps. Pieter is now once again a happy shooter, knowing he has access to a constant supply of ammunition his rifle likes.

Sometimes neck sizing can make the difference when you're looking for that last bit of accuracy. But the

(Photo courtesy Pieter Wolfe)

Cody Wolfe, Pieter's son, with his trophy Colorado elk, taken with handloaded 180-grain Swift Scirocco II shot from his dad's .300 Remington Ultra Magnum.

practice, as I've discussed previously, is reserved for bolt-action rifles only, as they alone have the mechanical advantage of being able to close the chamber on a cartridge with dimensions that are slightly larger than SAAMI specifications.

NEIGHBOR DAVE REVIVES A CLASSIC

This is a brief tale of a 1959 Colt Coltsman .300 Holland & Holland Magnum bolt-action rifle that has been passed around. I purchased it from Col. Le Frogg and didn't have an awful lot of time to develop a good load for it, so it sat in the cabinet. When my neighbor Dave offered to purchase the old girl from me, I agreed, knowing it would "stay in the family." Well, not only did neighbor Dave have her cleaned up and the stock bedded, he cooked up a load that is most impressive in a hunting rifle.

Using Reloder 22, Federal Large Rifle Magnum primers, and a 180-grain Swift Scirocco II, this gun printed a 1.2-inch three-shot group at 200 yards, during the previously mentioned "Handloaders Syndicate" competition. The 3-9x glass this rifle wears is on the light side for target shooting, but this gun is a shooter.

Velocities from this rifle are about 2,900 fps, which makes for a very flat-shooting, hard-hitting combination. A bit faster than the .30-06, yet with recoil that is very comfortable to manage from the bench, it makes a wonderful all-around caliber. The long, sloping shoulder of this classic case makes for very smooth feeding, and even though the rifle is more than a half-century old, it is with Dave's care and loading that it has truly come into its own. Dave uses it in the hunting fields with great effect, and I hope it sees many days afield. Old is not dead!

MARTY'S FAVORITE .270 LOAD

I have a customer who has a particularly finicky .270 Winchester. This gun didn't perform well with any factory ammunition, and the first trial handloads didn't help, either.

I don't shoot a .270 Winchester often, but my pal Marty Groppi does, and it's one of his favorites. So, I asked for some classified information: his pet handload recipe.

Marty obliged. The load uses a Sierra 130-grain spitzer and IMR4895, and while I've promised not to divulge the particulars, this load solved the problem for my customer. The formerly finicky rifle now prints three-shot groups just over MOA, and the client is very happy. Point is, keeping diligent records can help others when they have a problem rifle. Marty had spent the necessary time at the bench and found a load that worked well in four or five different .270 Winchesters, and that load proved to be a winner in my client's gun, as well.

***

From old guns to new, accuracy you can live with to accuracy you can be proud of, and problem guns turned to faithful treasures, these are the stories that handloading makes possible. Get involved, experiment, get *good* behind your rifle or handgun as only handloading can make you. After all, isn't that kind of success what we all want with our guns?

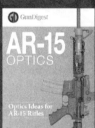
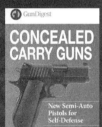

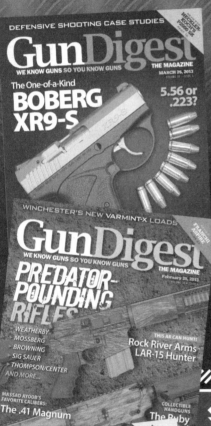